Mayfield's Quick View Guide to the Internet
for Anthropology

John W. Hoopes
University of Kansas
hoopes@ukans.edu

Jennifer Campbell
University of Tennessee, Knoxville

Michael Keene
University of Tennessee, Knoxville

Mayfield Publishing Company
Mountain View, California
London • Toronto

Acknowledgments

It is impossible to give credit here to the hundreds of individuals who have created the resources that have made this guide possible. The Internet has created a new community of scholars who freely interact with one another in the true spirit of cooperation. However, I would like to give special thanks to Allen Lutins and Anita Cohen-Williams, two dedicated scholars whose Internet indexes to anthropology blazed the trails for my own explorations of cyberspace. This work would not have been possible without their leadership.

International Standard Book Number 0-7674-1121-8

Manufactured in the United States of America
10 9 8 7 6 5 4

  This book is printed on recycled paper.

Mayfield Publishing Company
1280 Villa Street
Mountain View, California 94041

The Internet addresses listed in the text were accurate at the time of publication. The inclusion of a Web site does not indicate an endorsement by the authors or Mayfield Publishing Company, and Mayfield does not guarantee the accuracy of the information presented at these sites.

CONTENTS

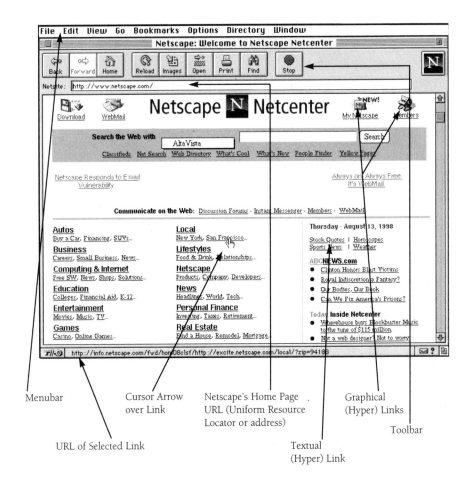

Menubar   Cursor Arrow   Netscape's Home Page   Graphical
               over Link   URL (Uniform Resource   (Hyper) Links
                              Locator or address)

                                               Toolbar

     URL of Selected Link   Textual
                                      (Hyper) Link

INTRODUCTION

What Can the Internet Do for You?

The Internet is a vast resource not only for information, entertainment, and interaction with other people in other places who share your interests, but also for learning. You can do everything from reading newspapers and magazines to learning how to create your own Web page, to videoconferencing, to watching video clips from your favorite movies, to downloading free software for your computer, to taking a virtual tour of Hawaii or a human heart. The Internet often has the most current news, the best views of weather anywhere, the best maps, and up-to-the-minute discussions of current events. Additionally, it is convenient to have a variety of dictionaries, thesauruses, and encyclopedias on hand while writing a paper.

Beyond all those uses, *the Internet frees you from the physical boundaries of your hometown, your campus, your city, your state, and your country.* Information from Japan or Germany or Australia can come to you just as fast and easily as information from across the hall. Because the Internet does not have opening or closing hours, its information is more accessible than the information in your library. It does not matter if your school's library is tiny; with access to the Internet, you have more information at your fingertips than the biggest library anywhere. All you need to do is learn how to find it. To help you find information on the Internet quickly and document it correctly is the purpose of this book.

What Are the Internet and the World Wide Web?

The Internet is a global network of computers. It is composed of many parts, such as Web documents, e-mail, Telnet, file transfer, Usenet (newsgroups), and Gopher. The Internet was user hostile until the **World Wide Web** came along. *The Web is a huge number of sites of information within the Internet.* Not only does the Web make accessing the Internet easier, but it also makes the Internet more fun because of the Web's **hypermedia** capabilities, such as audio, video, 3-D images, virtual reality, real-time communication, and animation. So let us help you get started!

QUICK VIEW
How Can I Use Graphical Access to the Internet?

Some students have access to computers that already have Netscape, Explorer, or some other graphical browser. If that's your situation, this page will get you off to a fast start. The rest of this guide will provide more detailed directions.

Using Netscape and Other Graphical Browsers

To access the Web's multimedia capabilities, you need a graphical **browser,** such as Netscape or Microsoft's Internet Explorer. (Note: You also need **TCP/IP** software; see page 4.) Netscape is used in the following description; other browsers, such as Explorer, work in essentially the same way.

Click on the Netscape icon to launch the program. The first Web page you see will depend on your **Internet service provider (ISP).** Most providers have designated a Web page to appear when you start Netscape. Many people like their first screen to be a search engine, such as Yahoo! <www.yahoo.com>. The Netscape Help button will show you how to change your start-up page.

There are several ways to access a **Web page** using Netscape. First, you can follow a **hyperlink,** which can be either text or an image. Textual hyperlinks, or **hypertext,** have a different look from the rest of the text. Depending on the browser you use, hypertext will either be a different color, or it will be underlined, or both. To follow a **link,** use your mouse to drag the arrow over the hypertext. When positioned over a link, the arrow will turn into a hand. Click the mouse, and you will go to that Web page. (Some links on some pages are not marked, but whenever your cursor arrow turns into a hand, you can click there and be taken somewhere else.)

Another option to clicking a link is to type out a page's address (called the **uniform resource locator,** or **URL**). Click on the Open button on the toolbar, type the URL in the box provided, and press Return. To navigate through a sequence of pages you have already seen, use the Back and Forward buttons on the toolbar. You may also access a Web page you have already seen by choosing it from your list of **bookmarks,** from entries on the History list (from the Window menu), or from the Go menu.

(Note: URLs in this book may be enclosed in angle brackets, < >, for readability. The brackets are not part of the address. Also note that the protocol "http://" is not included in the URLs listed here. Most browsers including Netscape and Microsoft Explorer automatically enter this for you.)

QUICK VIEW
HOW CAN I USE TEXT-ONLY ACCESS TO THE INTERNET?

Some students have access to computers that will give them only text from the Internet. If your computer gives you access to Lynx or some other text-only browser, this page will help you get off to a fast start. The rest of this guide provides more detailed instructions.

Using Lynx and Other Text-Only Browsers

Lynx is the most popular text-only browser. With text-only browsers, you cannot view the multimedia functions on the Web, such as pictures, audio, or video. You see only text. (Note: You do not need TCP/IP software to use Lynx.)

If you have a computer account at school, find out if it is a **UNIX** or VMS account. Chances are it will be a UNIX account. (Lynx runs on both, but our example shows how it works on UNIX.) Next, find out whether Lynx is available; if so, you can access Lynx by logging on to your computer account and then on to Lynx. After logging on, you will see either a $ or a %. Then type lynx. Your screen will look like this:

$ lynx

The first screen displayed should be a page containing information about the World Wide Web and giving you access to other pages.

To access a specific Web page, type lynx followed by the specific Web page's Internet address (its uniform resource locator, or URL). For example, if you wanted to go to Netscape's **home page**, your command line would look like this:

$ lynx http://www.home.netscape.com

When you view a Web page, the hypertext links (shortcuts to other pages) will appear in bold. To move your cursor to a link (in bold text), use your up- and down-arrow keys. When you place your cursor on the bold text, the text will become highlighted. To follow the link, press the right-arrow key. To go back, press the left-arrow key.

At the bottom of the screen, you will find a list of other commands. Simply type the first letter in the command name to execute that command. When you are finished, type q to quit. You will be asked if you really want to quit; type y for yes. This will bring you back to your system prompt (the $ or the %).

(Note: URLs in this book may be enclosed in angle brackets, < >, for readability. The brackets are not part of the address. Also note that the protocol "http://" is not included in the URLs listed here. You will have to add this when using Lynx.)

3

PART ONE
FINDING INFORMATION ON THE INTERNET

The Internet started in the 1960s as a project by the U.S. government to link supercomputers; eventually, its networking technology was used by academic institutions. In the beginning, the Internet was user hostile, and the numbers of computers and people it connected were limited. With the creation of the World Wide Web in the early 1990s by Tim Berners-Lee in Switzerland, the Internet became much more user friendly. Today, the Internet, a global network of computers, has a great many parts: the World Wide Web, Usenet, Gopher, Telnet, and FTP (file transfer protocol).

Technically, the World Wide Web is an Internet facility that uses hypertext to link multimedia sources. Web **servers** store files that can be viewed or down-loaded with a Web browser via **HTTP** (hypertext transfer protocol). The most popular text-only browser is Lynx; some popular graphical browsers are Netscape, Explorer, and AOL (America Online).

How the Internet Works—In Brief

To find the information you want, you should know a little about how your computer works with the Internet. That is the subject of the next five sections. If you are not interested in learning more about how computers work, you can skip to the section "How to Find the Information You Want" on page 7.

Hardware and Software

To gain access to the Internet, you need a computer with the appropriate hard-ware and software and an Internet service provider (ISP). Some popular ISPs are AOL, CompuServe, and Netcom. To access the Internet from home, you need a computer with a **modem** to connect your computer to the phone lines. Most modems run at 28.8K **bps** (bits per second). Faster modems can save you money if you are charged by the amount of time you spend on the Web. You will need a computer that has at least 8 MB (megabytes) of **RAM** (random-access memory). A **byte** is equal to 8 bits. (Note: You will also need to find out the networking capabilities your ISP; information is transferred only as fast as your ISP's slowest connection.)

For software, you will need TCP/IP (transmission control protocol/Internet protocol, or languages that allow computers to communicate with each other) to provide an interface between your computer and the Internet. If you have a Macintosh, you need MacTCP. If you have an IBM or clone, you need Winsock (which stands for "Windows socket"). Generally these networking protocols are already provided with your computer operating system. There are two main types of browsers: graphical and text-only, explained in more detail on pages 2 and 3.

Client/Server Systems

The Web works on a client/server system. The **client** is your computer and software; a server is any computer that houses files (text, audio, video, software) you want; and **networks** are systems that connect clients and servers. Think of your computer (the client) as a customer in a restaurant and the information provider (the server) as the chef. You order a meal (the information), and the waiter or waitress (the network) brings it back to you (your computer).

URLs and How They Work

To access a file by means of a Web browser, you must know its location. A URL (uniform resource locator), the Internet address for a file, is composed as follows:

```
protocol://server and domain name/file path/file
```

For example, suppose a student named Jane Smith at the University of Tennessee, Knoxville, has created a personal Web page for her résumé. The address for that page is as follows:

```
http://funnelweb.utcc.utk.edu/~jSmith/Resume.html
```

Here, http is the **protocol**; funnelweb.utcc.utk.edu is the server and **domain name**; ~jSmith is the **file path**; and Resume.html is the file. When we type this address in Netscape or Lynx, the browser reads the URL's components to find the specific page. Our computer has to know what kind of protocol, or language, to speak in order to communicate with the server. The first part of the URL not only tells us what type of file we are accessing, it also tells the computer what kind of language it needs to speak. In this case, we want a Web page in **HTML** (hypertext mark-up language), so the computer needs to speak hypertext, using HTTP (hypertext transfer protocol).

The next thing our computer needs to know is where the file is kept. This is what the second part of the URL, the server and domain name, tells us. The server where the Web page in this example is kept is called funnelweb. The funnelweb server is a computer at the University of Tennessee, Knoxville (UTK) that is denoted by utcc.utk.edu. The .edu lets us know that the domain is "educational." Other types of domains are .com for "commercial," .mil for "military," .org for "organizational," .net for "network," and .gov for "governmental" sites. Recently, seven new domain categories were added: .firm for "business," .store for "retail," .nom for "individual," .rec for "recreational," .info for "informational," .arts for "cultural," and .web for "Web-oriented" sites.

Of all the Web pages at UTK, how does your computer know which one is Jane Smith's? The last two parts of the URL tell how to get to Jane Smith's file. (Note the tilde symbol [~], which lets us know that we are looking for a personal page. This is not unique to UTK, but standard for many personal pages.) The user identification for Jane's file path, or "user area," is ~jSmith. The file we want is Resume.html. Now that our computer knows where to go, which file to get, and how to read it, the computer can display Jane Smith's page in Netscape. Notice that the file name has a mix of upper- and lowercase letters. Most URLs are case sensitive, so be sure to enter the URL exactly, including the uppercase letters. Note also that URLs never contain spaces.

Downloading Information

When you access a page, it sometimes takes a long time for the page to appear on your screen. If you are using Netscape and look at the bottom of the browser window while waiting for a Web page to appear, you should see a percentage of the amount of data transferred. When you access a Web page, a copy of the file is transferred to your computer's memory. This is called **downloading** a file. So, when you are **surfing** the Web, copies of all those Web pages are downloaded to your computer. However, the file is not downloaded all at once; it is transferred in pieces, or **packets.** Depending on the size of the files you are downloading, the length of time it takes for the Web page to appear will vary: A large Web page or a Web page with lots of graphics will slow the transfer. Image files are larger than text files and take longer to download. To shorten the download time in Netscape, turn off Auto Load Images (from the Options menu). To remove the check mark, click on Auto Load Images. To turn Auto Load Images back on, simply click on that line and it will be reactivated. By turning off Images, Web pages containing graphics will download faster, but you will not see any of the graphics automatically. To see the graphics individually, you have to click on the picture frame, or to see all the graphics at once, turn Auto Load Images back on and click on Reload (from the View menu) or on the Reload button on the toolbar.

Internet Service Providers (ISPs)

Before looking into commercial ISPs, check with your college's or university's computing center because some schools offer Internet services for home access to students, faculty, and staff. Internet services through your school will probably be the best deal. Although they may not always have the latest upgrades of hardware or software, the price will probably be hard to beat.

If you decide to go with a commercial ISP, you should do some comparison shopping. Think about what you will be using your Internet connection for, such as e-mail, Internet mail, graphical access to the Web, file transfer, Telnet, or storing Web pages. Once you decide what you will need, find out which ISPs offer all those services. After you have gathered a list of possible providers, ask some questions:

- What is the level of customer support, such as online help, user manuals, and telephone support (preferably 24 hours)?
- Is there an installation fee?
- Is there an extra cost for e-mail? If so, is the charge by message, by time, or by size of the message? Is there a storage fee for mail?
- Are there different rates for access at different times of the day?
- Is there a local dial-in number? Will long-distance fees be charged?
- What is the **bandwidth** (size of the bandwidth can affect access speed)?
- Is all the necessary software provided, such as TCP/IP and a browser (such as Netscape or Explorer)?
- Is storage space available for Web pages? If so, what is the charge?
- Are back-up servers available to help maintain continuous access?
- What kind of security is offered?

How to Find the Information You Want

The Internet is a vast and rapidly changing conglomeration of information. Finding your way to the particular piece of information you need can be difficult if you are not familiar with the search options available.

World Wide Web Search Engines

You can search the Web with **search engines** such as Yahoo! or AltaVista; you can search FTP archives with **Archie** and **ArchiePlex;** you can burrow through **Gopher** with **Veronica,** Archie, **Jughead,** and Gopher Jewels; and you can access library computers directly with Hytelnet <www.cam.ac.uk/Hytelnet/>. Sometimes the problem is *not finding enough information;* more often the problem is *finding too much information;* and always the problem is *finding the right information.* Here are some suggestions for solving these problems.

Search engines are computer programs that allow you to find the information you want through key word searches. The search engine provides a text box, into which you type key words associated with the information you want. Most search engines also offer more complex searches involving some variation of **Boolean logic** with the aid of "logical operators," such as AND, OR, and NOT. (Some search engines use a variation of Boolean searching by letting "+" stand for AND and "−" stand for NOT.) Some even offer more advanced searching, such as limiting your search to specific dates or ranking key words in order of appearance within the document.

There are hundreds of search engines for the Internet—too many to discuss here. Two popular and different types of search engines, Yahoo! (a searchable, browsable directory) and AltaVista (a powerful search engine), are briefly described below. For a more extensive list of search engines, see Netscape's list at <home.netscape.com/escapes/search/ntsrchdft-4.html>.

Yahoo! <www.yahoo.com>. Yahoo! is both a search engine and a directory made of subject trees. A **subject tree** is a hierarchical index system for finding information. You begin with a general subject, such as Medicine, and follow the subject tree's branches to a specific document. Yahoo!'s subject trees begin on its main page, which can be found at its URL.

Yahoo! is a good way to start searching because it looks at only a few key elements. Consequently, Yahoo! is the place to go for general discussions of your topic. To learn more about how to do a search on Yahoo!, click on the Options link located by the text box where you type in your key terms.

AltaVista <www.altavista.com>. Unlike Yahoo!, AltaVista does a thorough full-text search of documents for the key terms. If you put a fairly general key term into AltaVista, you will most likely receive hundreds or even thousands of links to pages that may only mention your topic in passing. AltaVista is a good place to search for obscure items or for very specific topics.

If you are getting too many hits for a topic on AltaVista, try doing the same search on Yahoo!; this should cut down the number of possible matches. Likewise, if you are searching on Yahoo! and you are not getting enough matches, try AltaVista.

AltaVista offers both a Simple Search and an Advanced Search. The Advanced Search helps you limit your results by specifying date ranges and ranking key terms. To find out more about Simple and Advanced Searches on AltaVista, click the Help button at the top of the first AltaVista page.

Searching via Key Words

Key word searches may require some imagination if you are not getting the results you hoped for. In most cases, your search was either too narrow or too broad. The tips below should help. Also, when you do find information you want, remember to check it for credibility. (See pages 12–14 on how to judge the reliability of Internet information.)

Narrowing a Search. If you are getting too many **hits** (successful key word matches), try narrowing your search by adding more key terms. Sometimes this will help, because most search engines will look for each of the terms independently but display the pages with the most matches first. Usually, you can narrow your search and make sure that all the key terms appear in the document by using AND between the key terms.

✓🖰 **Info Bit**—Narrow your search by looking for the most current information (or for the most relevant dates) in the AltaVista Advanced Search by entering a starting and ending date for the information.

✓🖰 **Info Bit**—Some search engines, such as Yahoo!, allow you to search within document titles only. This will narrow your search results and may give you better sources on your topic.

Broadening a Search. If you are not getting enough hits, broaden your search by deleting some of the more specific key terms or substituting synonyms for the key words you already have listed. For example, for a search about how to make a Web page, try several search strings, such as "Web page design," "creating a Web page," and "making a Web page." Also, you may want to try a more general category under which your topic falls. For example, if you want information on the Hopi god Kokopeli, but you get only one or two hits, try searching for "Hopi religion" or just "Hopi."

✓🖰 **Info Bit**—The Web is a big place with millions of documents, and it is growing by the hour. No single search engine can cover the whole Web, because each search engine covers different, although overlapping, territory. If your search does not work with the first engine you use, try running it on several different ones.

✓🖰 **Info Bit**—Some search engines are designed to find specific topics, such as Law Crawler at <www.lawcrawler.com> or the Amazing Environmental Organization Web Directory at <www.webdirectory.com>.

Finding Phrases. If you want to find documents containing a specific phrase, such as "Green Bay Packers," put the phrase in double quotation marks to lock them together. Otherwise, you will get thousands of pages that have only "green" or "bay" or "packers" in them.

Searching via Subject Trees

As described previously in the section on Yahoo!, a subject tree is a hierarchical index of topics that allows you to begin with a broad category and follow the subject tree's branches down to a specific file. Subject trees can be good places to start your search because you can get an idea of the different types of information available on your topic.

One of the first and best subject trees is The Virtual Library <vlib.org/Home. html>. There are different ways to search The Virtual Library. You can start searching the Subject Index on the main page, or you can search the Category Subtree.

ᴗ🖰 Info Byte: *Some Common Error Messages*

Connection refused by server

Server is busy. The maximum number of simultaneous connections has probably been reached. Try again later.

Document contains no data

First, try clicking the link again. If this doesn't work, there may be a glitch in the network.

Error 400

Your request could not be understood by the server. Your Web browser may be malfunctioning or your Internet connection may be unreliable. Try shutting down and restarting your computer.

Forbidden access (Error 401)

For some reason, the creator or maintainer of a page does not want any "outside" visitors, and he or she has restricted the access to the page.

No DNS entry

Means "No Domain Name System," or that the server does not exist. If you are linking to the page from another, try clicking the link again. If you are entering the URL, make sure you have entered it correctly—with any capital letters and without spaces. If the URL is correct, the server may not be working.

No response

There may be too many connections, or the server may be down for some reason. Try again later.

Not found (Error 404)

The file you are looking for is not on this server. It may have been moved or deleted.

Transfer interrupted!

For some reason, the server was not able to transfer all the data for this page. Try reloading.

Other Protocols: Telnet and Gopher

Web servers communicate through HTTP (hypertext transfer protocol), but there are other, older information systems, such as Telnet and Gopher, that communicate through other protocols. The URLs for these other Internet systems begin with a different protocol abbreviation, or prompt, such as `ftp://`, `gopher://`, or `telnet://`. Telnet and Gopher are described here; FTP (file transfer protocol) is discussed in Part Two.

Telnet. Some electronic **bulletin boards,** library catalogs, and school computer accounts are not part of the Web. To access these sources, you need to use **Telnet,** a protocol that lets you communicate with computers that use the UNIX operating system. To use Telnet, you need to log on to another computer (a remote host). When you log on, a text-only screen identical to the screen of the remote host will appear. Then you can issue commands from your computer and have them carried out by the remote host.

A Telnet session's first screen usually lists instructions for logging on, accessing the Help page, and logging off. If you get a blank screen, try pressing Enter (or Return). If you get a screen with instructions, *read it carefully,* because when you want to exit a session, you may not remember how. If no instructions are given, try typing ? and pressing Enter to get the Help page. To exit, hold the Command key and type q if you are using a Macintosh, or hold the Control key and type q if you are using a PC.

To use Telnet, you will need Telnet software. If your ISP does not provide the software, you can download it from the Internet for free. For a Macintosh, get NCSA Telnet at <www.ncsa.uiuc.edu/SDG/Software/Brochure/Overview/MacTelnet. overview.html>. For a PC, get EWAN Telnet from ZDNet at <www5.zdnet.com>. On the screen that appears, click on the Downloads link. Type EWAN in the key word box and click on the Search button.

Gopher. Gopher is a menu-driven information system started at the University of Minnesota and named after its mascot, a gopher. It is a predecessor of the World Wide Web. However, Gopher menu systems and files can be accessed via the Web. There is a lot of good information on Gopher that is not available elsewhere on the Internet. If you want to search Gopher, a good place to start is with Gopher Jewels at <galaxy.einet.net/GJ/>. Gopher Jewels catalogs many Gopher sites by subject tree. For a more thorough search of Gopher sites, use a search engine, such as Jughead (document title search) or Veronica (full-text search). For a list of Jughead servers, go to <www.yahoo.com/Computers_and_Internet/ Internet/Gopher/Searching/Jughead>. To learn more about Veronica, see the **Frequently Asked Questions (FAQs)** page at <gopher://gopher.scs.unr.edu/ 00/veronica/veronica-faq>. To search using Veronica, go to <gopher://gopher.scs. unr.edu/11/veronica>.

How to Judge the Reliability of Internet Information

Students who are accustomed to doing research in libraries face new issues when they start doing research on the Internet. Before a book or journal appears in a university library, it has usually gone through a number of checks to make sure the information in it is reliable. For example, if you find a copy of *Moby Dick* in your university library, you can be sure you are getting a generally accepted version of the real thing. But if you find a copy of *Moby Dick* on the Internet, you need to give some thought to *where you found it,* whether the person who put it on the Internet is a *reliable authority on the subject* (someone who can be trusted not to enter his or her own personal, political, or scholarly biases into the text), and whether your professor will *accept your judgment* of the reliability of that material.

Arguably, student researchers should always make these decisions, even about materials they find in the university library. However, judging the reliability of sources found on the Internet is crucial because there is no regulating body that monitors the reliability of what is on the Internet. Although there is so much information on the Internet that it can seem like a university library, it is actually more like a huge open-air market. In one corner there might be reliable sources from whom you can obtain valuable information. But over in another corner there might be weirdos, wackos, and eccentrics, from whom anything you obtain is, at best, questionable. The problem is that on the Internet there is no way to tell the difference. Someone who wants to turn *Moby Dick* into a glorification of bloodsports or an animal rights tract can post a rewritten version with no indication of its differences from Melville's original. There's a saying in Latin, *caveat emptor,* or "let the buyer beware." When it comes to doing your research on the Internet, the saying should be *caveat internauta,* or "let the surfer beware."

Here is a list of points to consider when you are trying to judge the reliability of information you find on the Internet:

- **Who is the author or sponsor of the page?** On the page you are citing, or on a page linked to it, that individual or organization should be identified, that individual's qualifications should be apparent, and other avenues of verification should be open to you. For a good example of a reliable source, see the "Notes about this document" area for the hypertext version of *Pride and Prejudice* at <www.pemberley.com/janeinfo/pridprej.html>. A page created by a person or an organization that does not provide this information is not a good source to cite.

- **Are there obvious reasons for bias?** If the page is presented by a tobacco company consortium, you should be suspicious of its reports on the addictiveness of nicotine. Is there any advertising? If the page is sponsored by

Acme Track Shoes, you should be suspicious of its claims for Acme track shoes' performance.

- **Is contact information provided?** If the only identification available is something cryptic, such as "Society for Feruginous Retorts," be suspicious of the page's reliability. If the page is sponsored by a reputable person or organization, there should be some other way to verify that reputation, such as an e-mail or postal address. (Note: A tilde [~] in the page's address usually indicates a personal home page and may require more searching for reliability.)

- **Is there a copyright symbol on the page?** If so, who holds the copyright?

- **Is this page a "zombie,"** or one considered "walking dead" because the person who posted it no longer maintains or updates it? Even though the information is "alive" in that it is still accessible, it is "dead" in that it could well be several years old! Many pages have a "last updated" date.

- **What is the purpose of the page?** Why is this information being posted—as information, as a public service, as a news source, as a research tool for academics, as a personal ax to grind, or as a way to gain attention?

- **How well organized is the page?** Is the page easy to navigate? Is it complete?

- **Is the information on the page *primary* or *secondary*?** That is, is it a report of facts, such as a medical researcher's article describing a new drug treatment for HIV infection, thus making it primary information, or is it an Internet newsgroup discussion about the new drug treatment, thus making it secondary information? The papers and reports you write for your college classes need to be based on primary information whenever possible. The further away from the primary sources your own sources are, the less reliable the information is.

- **Can you verify the information** on the Web page in some other way? For example, can you check the page's bibliography (if there is one) against your library's holdings or check the information against a source in the library?

- **If you are worried that the information may lack credibility, try starting with a source you know is reputable.** For example, if you have to do a project on the latest in cancer research, you can begin your search at major cancer research institutes, such as Mayo Clinic in Rochester, Minnesota <www.mayo.edu>.

- Finally, remember that **even though a page might not meet your standards as a citable source, it may help you generate good ideas** or point to other usable sources. Also, be sure not to stop your search at the first page you find—shop around and do some comparing so that you can have points of reference.

Ultimately, the problem with reliability of information on the Web is like the whispering game children play. Someone whispers a message to the first child, who whispers it to the second, and so on. By the time it gets to the last child, the message is hopelessly distorted. Web pages can work the same way when people get their information from other people's Web pages: The first person who posts information may make a few small errors; the second unintentionally repeats them and makes one or two more; the third makes a few more; and so on. For information seekers it can be impossible to tell where in the chain the information is coming from, but that makes a difference in the information's reliability. Remember: It never hurts to check against a library reference.

How to Document Information from Electronic Sources

Whenever you are doing research and writing for a classroom assignment, documenting your sources correctly is important. If the information, ideas, or other kinds of materials (such as drawings and graphics) in your paper are from a source, you need to let your readers know by adding appropriate documentation. (And if you quote passages, you need to add quotation marks or make block quotations as well.) The documentation you provide needs to be complete enough that a reader who wants to check your sources will be able to find them. Material from the Internet and other electronic sources, just like print sources, must be properly documented.

Portable versus Online Sources

There are two kinds of electronic sources of information—*unchangeable* and *changeable*—and they need to be documented in slightly different ways.

Unchangeable (or Portable) Sources. Suppose you go to the library (or access its collections on a remote computer) and look up material on a **CD-ROM** (compact disk with read-only memory), such as InfoTrac or some other portable database. As an electronic source, the CD-ROM is stable—that is, anyone could look at it today, next month, or next year, and find the same information. It has a date and place of publication (although here "publication" actually means "production") and a version number, which should be shown in your documentation just as they would be for a journal article. Thus, for unchangeable sources there is no need to add extra elements to your documentation.

Changeable (or Online) Sources. For materials you find on the Internet, you need to add some information to your documentation. Usually, it includes the date you accessed the information and its URL. Sometimes, you may be required to include the path you took to get to the page or even a hard copy (a printout) of the page. If information you find on the Internet is crucial to your work, it is always a good idea to print out a hard copy, just in case.

Different Styles for Different Fields

If you are taking a freshman or sophomore English composition class, your teacher may require you to use the Modern Language Association (MLA) style, which is what literature and language specialists use. Or you may be given the choice of either MLA style or American Psychological Association (APA) style, which is what academics in the social sciences (such as psychology or sociology) generally use. When documenting Web and Internet sources, many teachers recommend the Alliance for Computers in Writing (ACW) style <www.cas.usf.edu/english/walker/mla.html>. Professors for higher-level classes or classes in other fields may expect you to use some other style—the Council of Biology Editors (CBE) style is used in the life sciences; the *Chicago Manual of Style* (CMS) is used in business, history, and many hard sciences; or even the Institute of Electrical and Electronic Engineers (IEEE) style <www.ieee.org/webdoc.html>, which is used in fields such as computer science. Although there are hundreds of different styles, the right one for you will probably look close to one of the four varieties presented here.

When and What to Document

Here are six simple guidelines to help you decide when and what to document:

1. If you use the exact language of your source, you must use quotation marks and cite the source.

2. Use direct quotations only if there is something unique about your source's language or if your own words will not do the job better.

3. Directly quote only as much as you need—the bare minimum.

4. If you use information that is not common knowledge, you must cite the source. If this information would not be familiar to someone who had not researched the subject, it is not common knowledge and its source must be cited.

5. Cite all kinds of borrowed information, not just words and facts. Sources can also include drawings, photos, artwork, ideas, music—anything you use that is not yours.

6. To work your quoted or otherwise borrowed material into the text more smoothly, introduce it with the name of the source. To introduce your borrowed material, use a tag line—for example, "As Stanley Prusiner, one of the leading authorities on communicable diseases, said . . ."

Modern Language Association (MLA) Author-Page Style

MLA style uses parenthetical citations within the text. They lead readers to a list of entries at the end of the document called *Works Cited.* Generally, the material within the parenthetical citation includes the author's name and the page number to which you are referring. Here we summarize briefly the MLA style of documentation, and on the next page we go into more detail about the MLA style for citing electronic sources. If you want more details about MLA documentation style, consult the *MLA Handbook for Writers of Research Papers,* 4th edition (1995). A basic MLA citation in the text will look like this:

```
. . . leads to better research (Morring 57).
```

This citation would lead readers to the following entry at the end of the document:

```
Morring, Frank, Jr. "Russian Hardware Allows Earlier
     Space Station Experiments." Aviation Week and
     Space Technology 16 (May 1994): 57.
```

Citations in the Text

In MLA style, parenthetical citations go at the end of the sentence in which the source material appears. If the sentence already includes the author's name, then only the page number appears in the parenthetical citation. In the case of more than one work by the same author, a short title is added in the parentheses. The page number is given in the parentheses, without *p.* or *pp.*

Parenthetical citations for direct quotations in the text appear after the closing quotation marks but before the final punctuation. Direct quotations that are more than four lines long should be indented an inch, rather than being enclosed in quotation marks. The parenthetical reference for such quotations follows the quotation's final punctuation.

Entries in the Works Cited List

The list of works cited includes only sources mentioned in the text and not all sources consulted. Entries are arranged alphabetically by the author's last name (or by the first significant word in the title if there is no author). The page is double spaced, with the first line of each entry flush left and subsequent lines indented half an inch (or five spaces on a typewriter). The basic pattern of an entry is author's name, title, and publication information (place, name of publisher, date, and page numbers).

MLA Style for Citing Electronic Sources

The MLA style for citing electronic sources is still evolving. Presented here is information from the current *MLA Handbook* (4th edition) as supplemented by *The Mayfield Handbook of Technical and Scientific Writing.*

CD-ROMs and Other Portable Databases

For unchangeable sources, the citation in the *Works Cited* list includes the author, title, and date information just as for print documents. After the title of the database, there is a period, followed by identification of the medium (such as CD-ROM), another period, and the producer's name and date of the product.

```
Morring, Frank, Jr. "Russian Hardware Allows Earlier
    Space Station Experiments." Aviation Week and
    Space Technology 16 (May 1994): 57. InfoTrac:
    General Periodicals Index. CD-ROM. Information
    Access. Aug. 1996.
```

Online Sources

For changeable sources, use this format: author's name, full title (articles in quotation marks, books underlined) and any larger document of which it is a part, date of publication or most recent revision (if available), the full URL address enclosed in angle brackets (< >), and the date accessed enclosed in parentheses. Here are two examples:

```
Shepherdson, Charles. "History and the Real: Foucault
    with Lacan." Postmodern Culture 5.2 (Jan. 1995):
    <http://jefferson.village.virginia.edu/pmc/
    shepherd.195.html> (15 May 1995).

Harnack, Andrew, and Gene Kleppinger. "Beyond the MLA
    Handbook: Documenting Electronic Sources on the
    Internet." Kairos 1.2 (1996): <http://english.
    ttu.edu/kairos/1.2> (10 Oct. 1996).
```

Ideally, the URL should not be interrupted by a line break; however, if it is too long to fit on one line, break the URL after a period or slash. Do not put a period after the URL. The same form is used for a document retrieved from a file transfer protocol (FTP) archive, except the abbreviation ftp precedes the address, and the URL is not enclosed in angle brackets.

American Psychological Association (APA) Author-Date Style

APA style places the author's name and date of publication within parentheses in the text, linked to a list of references (titled *References*) at the end of the document. Although the focus of this guide is electronic sources, here is a brief overview of APA documentation style. For more information, consult the *Publication Manual of the American Psychological Association*, 4th edition (1994).

Citations in the Text

Citations in the text generally include the author's last name and the year in parentheses. So a citation to something by Bill Jones in 1988 would be (Jones, 1988). The parenthetical citation precedes the sentence's final punctuation. If the author's name has already appeared in the sentence, the year of publication follows it in parentheses. APA requires page numbers only if you are citing a direct quotation or a specific table, figure, or equation. If you need to include page numbers (and some teachers want page numbers for everything), use *p.* or *pp.*

Parenthetical citations for direct quotations in the text appear after the closing quotation marks but before the final punctuation. If the quotation is more than forty words long, it should be indented an inch. If the quotation is set off, the citation appears after the quotation's final punctuation.

Entries in the References List

Each entry in the reference list must match a citation, and the entire list must be double spaced. The entries should be alphabetized by the author's last name and, in the case of multiple entries by one author, listed chronologically, beginning with the earliest. APA recommends that the first line of each entry be indented one inch (or five to seven spaces) when materials are submitted for publication, but in APA publications, the first line is flush left and subsequent lines are indented. Each entry has four elements: author, date, title, and publication information. A typical entry for a book looks like this:

Insel, P. M., & Roth, W. T. (1998). <u>Core concepts in health</u> (8th ed.). Mountain View, CA: Mayfield.

APA Style for Citing Electronic Sources

APA's style for citing electronic sources is still evolving. The basic citation has five elements: author, date, title, document type, and publication information. The information here has been supplemented by the extension of APA made in *The Mayfield Handbook of Technical and Scientific Writing*.

CD-ROMs and Other Portable Databases

If you use information from a CD-ROM or other unchangeable source (such as a magnetic tape or commercially produced disk), you need to name the author, date, and title just as for a print source. In square brackets after the title, identify the electronic medium. At the end of the entry, give the source location and name of the producer. A typical entry looks like this (because there is no author in this example, the publication's name comes first):

> The world factbook 1994 [CD-ROM]. (1994).
> Washington, DC: Central Intelligence Agency [Producer and distributor].

You may encounter a CD-ROM version of a document that is also available in hard copy. If so, your citation needs to include information for both (while making it clear that you accessed the CD-ROM version). This note is for an abstract that was read on CD-ROM:

> Morring, F., Jr. (1994, May 16). Russian hardware allows earlier space station experiments [CD-ROM]. Aviation Week & Space Technology, 140, 57. Abstract from: InfoTrac General Periodicals Index-A: Abstract 15482317.

Online Sources

For changeable sources, use this format: author's name, date of the most recent revision (if available), title of the source, and identification of the type of document (such as online serial or personal home page). In place of a publisher is the complete URL, underlined. If the URL will not fit on one line, break it after a period or slash. Finally, the entry includes in parentheses the date you visited that page. Here is an example:

> Land, T. (1996, March 31). Web extension to American Psychological Association style (WEAPAS) [WWW document] (Rev. 1.2.4). URL http://www.beadsland.com/ weapas/ (visited 1997, April 24).

Council of Biology Editors (CBE) Citation-Sequence System

The CBE style manual presents two systems of documentation. The one summarized here uses numbers in the text that refer to a numbered list of references at the end of the document. Because our purpose here is to show how CBE treats electronic sources, we summarize only the citation-sequence system. For full details, refer to *Scientific Style and Format: The CBE Manual for Authors, Editors, and Publishers,* 6th edition (1994).

Citations in the Text

When a source is first used in the text, it is assigned a number that it retains whenever it is used again. The number appears in superscript immediately after the source is referred to, not separated by a space. If more than one source is cited, the numbers are separated by commas without spaces. Here is a typical entry (taken from *The Mayfield Handbook of Technical and Scientific Writing*):

```
     The oncogene jun has presently become one of the
best-known oncogenes because of its ability to act as
a transcription factor[1]. One study[2] examined . . .
```

Entries in the References List

Titled *References* or *Cited References,* the whole list is double spaced. The sequence is established by the order in which the items appear in the text. The number of the entry is not indented and is followed by a period. Each entry has four basic elements: author, title, publication information, and page numbers. Authors' first and middle names are abbreviated, as are other elements, and the abbreviations are not followed by periods. Here is an example of a journal article entry:

```
1. Lenski RE, May RM. The evolution of virulence in
   parasites and pathogens: reconciliation between
   two competing hypotheses. J Theoret Biol 1994;
   169:253-65.
```

Here is a typical entry for a book:

```
13. Mandelbrot BB. The fractal geometry of nature.
    San Francisco: WH Freeman; 1995. 460 p.
```

CBE Style for Citing Electronic Sources

The CBE style for citing electronic sources is still evolving. The pattern for online sources recommended here is taken from *The Mayfield Handbook of Technical and Scientific Writing* and is consistent with other CBE formats.

CD-ROMs and Other Portable Databases

For unchangeable sources, the author, date, and title information is provided just as for a print source. In brackets after the title, identify the medium. At the end of the entry, include the name of the database and its location. Here is a typical entry:

> 9. Morring F Jr. Russian hardware allows earlier space station experiments [CD-ROM]. Aviat Wk Space Technol 1994;140:57. Abstract from: InfoTrac General Periodicals Index-A: Abstract 15482317.

Online Sources

The *CBE Manual* does not require the full Internet address for changeable sources. Nonetheless, it makes sense to include this additional information. Here is a sample entry with the URL and date of access added:

> 1. Brooker MIH, Slee AV. New taxa and some new nomenclature in Eucalyptus. Muelleria [abstract online] 1996; 9(75-85). Available from WWW; <http://155.187.10.12/cpbr/publications/brooker-slee2.html> (Accessed 1997 Feb 13.)

Note that the type of online document is named and the date of access is provided.

Chicago Manual of Style *(CMS) Superscript System*

Three documentation systems are presented in *The Chicago Manual of Style*, 14th edition (1993). The one shown here uses superscript numbers, keyed to numbered endnotes or footnotes. It is based on an adaptation of CMS style for college writers: *A Manual for Writers of Term Papers, Theses, and Dissertations*, 6th edition, by Kate Turabian (1996).

Citations in the Text

Note numbers that appear in the text are superscript numbers. They normally go at the end of the sentence, following the final punctuation; if they must be used within a sentence, they should go after a punctuation mark. CMS superscript notations in the text will look like this:

```
One literary critic notes "Austen's uncertainty about
the inner life of Darcy,"¹ and another explains that
Austen's novels, like those of many other nineteenth-
century British authors, empower their heroines "over
their own plot" and place them at the center of the
action.²
```

If you use a direct quotation in the text, the note number appears after the closing quotation marks. A direct quotation that is eight lines or more should be set off, single spaced, and indented four spaces. The note number appears right after the quotation's final punctuation.

Entries in the Notes List

Each entry in the list of notes should correspond to a superscript number in the text. The entries are arranged numerically, with the reference number followed by a period and a space. The entire list of notes should be double spaced, with the first line of each entry indented half an inch.

Each entry generally has four elements: author, title, publication information, and page numbers. The author's name is given in normal order (first name, then last name). Here is a basic entry for a book:

```
    2. Hilary M. Lips, Sex and Gender: An
Introduction, 3rd ed. (Mountain View, CA: Mayfield
Publishing, 1997), 151.
```

If note number 3 were to that same source, just a different page, the entry would read

```
    3. Ibid., 159.
```

CMS Style for Citing Electronic Sources

The CMS style for citing electronic sources is still evolving. The pattern for unchangeable sources presented here comes from the current (14th) edition. The pattern for changeable sources comes from the adaptation of CMS style by Kate Turabian (cited on the previous page). An excellent online source for more information about adapting CMS style for online documents is Maurice Crouse's paper "Citing Electronic Information in History Papers," available at <www.people.memphis.edu/~mcrouse/elcite.html>.

CD-ROMs and Other Portable Databases

For unchangeable electronic sources, the citation is like that for print sources, with the addition of the name of the producer or vendor and any access numbers associated with the document. Here is a sample entry:

> 1. Frank Morring, Jr., "Russian Hardware Allows
> Earlier Space Station Experiments," <u>Aviation Week &
> Space Technology,</u> 16 May 1994, 57; Abstract 15482317:
> InfoTrac General Periodicals Index-A [CD-ROM],
> September 1996.

Online Sources

For changeable sources, the entry contains the usual elements for print sources, followed by an indication in square brackets of what type of document it is, the complete document address, and the date of access.

> 2. Charles Shepherdson, "History and the Real:
> Foucault with Lacan," <u>Postmodern Culture</u> 5, no. 2
> (January 1995) [serial online]; available from
> http://jefferson.village.virginia.edu/pmc/shepherd.
> 195.html; Internet; accessed 15 May 1995.

PART TWO
COMMUNICATING ON THE INTERNET

Part One of this guide explained some of the most important ways people use the Internet to find information. The subject of this part is how to use the Internet to communicate with other people. Of course, making a distinction between these two activities is misleading. For example, when you join an e-mail listserv on the subject of technical communication <listserv@listserv.okstate.edu> because you want to learn more about the field and maybe find an internship, your primary motive may be communication, but you are certainly also finding information.

Communicating on the Internet takes many forms. Here is an overview of the topics discussed in this section:

- E-mail—How to send e-mail to your friends all over the world, how to read e-mail addresses, and how to use Internet mail.

- Netiquette—What you should and shouldn't do when you are communicating on the Internet.

- Discussion groups—How to subscribe to listserv mailing lists (and how to unsubscribe); how to take part in Usenet newsgroups.

- Real-time communication—What is Internet Relay Chat (IRC); what are MOOs, MUDs, MUSHes, and WOOs; what is videoconferencing?

- Electronic file transfer—An introduction to file transfer protocol (FTP) and how to do it.

- Risks and precautions—Find out what you need to know about computer security, disclosing personal information, copyright, libel, plagiarism, and viruses.

How to Communicate with E-Mail

E-mail is a way of sending messages electronically. If you get e-mail service through an ISP, you will be given a mailbox and software for reading and storing your mail, for composing and sending messages, and for creating mailing lists. There are lots of different e-mail software packages available, but they all work in much the same way. Most Web browsers such as Netscape and Explorer have built-in e-mail software.

When someone sends you a message, it will be temporarily stored on your ISP's mail server. You will use your e-mail software to see if you have any messages waiting. If you do, the e-mail software will download them from the mail server to your computer, where you can read, store, delete, reply to, print, or forward them.

When you get an e-mail account, you will be given an e-mail address. The address has three parts: for example, user_name@domain_name. Usually, you will be able to create your own user name, which is how your mailbox is identified. The *at* sign (@) separates the user name from the domain name. The domain name is the name of the computer or system where your e-mail is stored.

In the above e-mail address "user_name" and "domain_name" have no spaces (which is indicated by the underscore)—e-mail addresses cannot have any spaces. The address is also in all lowercase, because e-mail addresses are not case sensitive and are easier to read and type without caps. If you get mail returned because the address could not be found, make sure you have entered it correctly. If you have, and the mail is still returned, the person may have changed addresses or may be having problems with the mail system.

Internet Mail

Internet mail (e-mail sent over the Internet) takes e-mail a step further. For example, suppose you are surfing the Web and find a page that has great information, and you want to get in touch with the person who created the page. Usually the person who created the page will include a link for sending e-mail. When you click the link, a window will appear where you can type and send a message. However, you need **SMTP** (simple mail transfer protocol) to send the message. Check with your ISP for the name of its SMTP server. To receive Internet e-mail, you will also need a **POP** (post office protocol) server. Check with your ISP for a list of services to see if POP mail accounts are available.

Virtual Communities: Listservs and Newsgroups

Virtual communities are ways of organizing or connecting people of like interests over the Internet. In the following section we discuss some modes of communication that are analogous to print newsletters.

Listserv Mailing Lists

Listservs are servers that house **mailing lists.** Listserv mailing lists are discussion groups categorized by special interest. Unlike Usenet newsgroups, which let you browse messages posted on Usenet (discussed next), listserv mail messages are sent directly to your e-mail address. When a member posts a message to the listserv, the message is delivered to every subscriber.

When you subscribe, your name and e-mail address are added to the mailing list. From that point on, you will receive all e-mail messages that are posted to the group. It is always wise to **lurk** (hang out and just read messages) for a while before joining the discussion. When you reply to an e-mail message from a listserv, you can either mail the person who sent the message originally or you can post your response to the entire group.

Info Byte: Netiquette

As with all human communities, even virtual ones, there is acceptable and unacceptable behavior. **Netiquette,** the guidelines for communicating with others on the Internet, helps us all respect the people who share our cyberspace. Most netiquette guidelines are just common sense, a reminder that even though we're in cyberspace, our relations with others are still human relations. Here are some tips:

- Do not use foul or abusive language.

- Do not force offensive material on unwilling participants.

- Do not join in **flaming** (by sending cruel e-mail to someone). Usually, flaming is started over not-so-common-sense breaches of netiquette.

- Do not shout (that is, do not use all caps) at other people on the Internet.

- Do not take off on tangents that are too far from a discussion group's stated purpose.

- Do not post ambiguous questions or ask questions that are answered in a group's Frequently Asked Questions (FAQs) list.

- Be careful to avoid **spamming,** or sending the same message (like a sales pitch) to many different addresses, especially listservs. Spamming is the equivalent of junk mail and will get you flamed in no time.

- Reread your Internet messages before sending them. Something written in haste may be misread.

One way to find a listserv for people with a particular interest is to do a key word search on a search engine, such as Yahoo! or AltaVista, by entering the topic and the word `listserv`. Or you can use search engines that are specifically designed for listservs, such as Inter-Links at <alabanza.com/ kabacoff/Inter-Links/listserv.html>. Another good place to search or browse already extensive lists of mailing lists categorized by subject is CataList, the official catalog of LISTSERV lists, at <www.lsoft.com/catalist.com>.

To subscribe to a list, send an e-mail message to the listserv address. Do not put anything in the subject line of the message. Then, on the first line of the body of the message, type the following:

```
subscribe [list name] [your full name]
```

Once you subscribe, you will receive a set of instructions for list members. It will tell you where to post messages (usually a different address than the subscription address) and what subscription options you have (such as "digest," which combines each day's postings into one packet, or "unsubscribe"). Be sure to save this message!

To unsubscribe, send an e-mail message to the listserv subscription address. Again, do not put anything in the subject line of the message. Then, on the first line of the body of the message, type the following:

```
unsubscribe [list name] [your full name]
```

Remember to unsubscribe if you terminate your e-mail account. Only you can unsubscribe your name from a list.

Usenet Newsgroups

Usenet is a computer network accessible on the Internet that is mainly used for discussion groups. **Newsgroups** are discussion groups on Usenet organized by interest categories. Basically, newsgroups are sets of archived messages, articles, or postings. You are free to browse any newsgroup's articles.

To access newsgroups, you need a newsreader. Most graphical browsers, such as Netscape and Explorer, come equipped with a newsreader. The next thing you need to know is the Network News Transfer Protocol (NNTP) server. Contact your ISP to find out the name of its NNTP server.

Newsgroups have many **threads** of discussion. A thread is the original message that begins a discussion and all of the replies to that message. Most browsers have options for following threads. For example, when you pull up a newsgroup article in Netscape, there are links at the top of the article to all of the messages in that thread.

Newsgroup articles can literally be here today and gone tomorrow. Because of the thousands of articles a newsgroup can receive in a day, old articles are deleted to make room for the new ones. Depending on how busy a newsgroup is, articles may be deleted within several hours. If you find an article you may want to refer to later, save or print a copy, because it may not be there the next time you look. To save a document as a file on your computer's hard drive, select Save from the File menu and choose a destination.

When accessing newsgroups, some of your basic options are to browse, read, or save newsgroup messages; to reply only to the person who posted a message or to the entire newsgroup; or to post a new message that starts a thread of discussion. Most newsreaders will have buttons for each of these options. As with listservs, it is a good idea to lurk on a newsgroup before you become an active member. To get an idea of what kinds of topics are appropriate, find out if the newsgroup has a FAQs (Frequently Asked Questions) page. Newsgroup members will become irate if you post questions that are already discussed in the FAQs, and they will not appreciate messages that discuss topics beyond the scope of their newsgroup. If you make either of these mistakes, you could get flamed—bombarded with irate mail messages! (See Info Byte: Netiquette, page 26.)

Virtual Communities: Real-Time Communication

Real-time communication is different from the various forms of delayed communication that we have discussed so far—e-mail, listservs, and newsgroups. In real time, your messages—whether text, audio, or video—are seen almost instantaneously by those on your channel, instead of being sent and read later by the recipient. There are two main methods of real-time communication—chat groups via Internet Relay Chat (**IRC**) and multi-user domains (**MUDs, MOOs, MUSHes,** etc.).

To participate in real-time communication, you need some special software. Chat groups, MUDs, MOOs, and videoconferences all require different software; sometimes, different software is even required from chat room to chat room, from MUD to MUD, and so on. This section provides an overview of some of the real-time communication options, as well as links to some Web sites to help you get started. And remember the same netiquette (see page 26) for other forms of communication is still in effect in real time. For example, avoid shouting (addressing people in all caps), and be careful not to divulge too much personal information.

Internet Relay Chat

Internet Relay Chat (IRC) is a protocol that gives you the ability to communicate in real time with people worldwide through **chat** groups. Once you have the proper software in place, you can connect to an IRC server. After you are connected to the server, you can sign on to one of the channels and communicate with others who are signed on to the same channel. You can have a public conversation, where everyone on the channel is included, or a private conversation between you and one other person. Remember, though, that in IRC channels, the channel moderator can kick you off and refuse you future access, so follow netiquette.

A good place to begin is with a document called The IRC Prelude, available at <www.irchelp.org>. Useful software that you can download is mIRC (a graphical client) at <www.mirc.co.uk>. This page also provides IRC FAQs.

MUDs, MOOs, MUSHes, and WOOs

The first multi-user programming option was the Multi-User Domain (Dimension or Dungeon), or MUD. A MUD is a computer program that creates a world for users to log on to (usually by Telnet). Users can participate in role-playing, assuming various characters or personae. The next to come along were the MUD Object-Oriented environment, or MOO, and the Multi-User Shared Hallucination, or MUSH. MOOs, MUSHes, and other multi-user domains are similar. They all have a gathering of users, usually role-playing, but MOOs and MUSHes allow for physical objects to be placed in the virtual room where the participants are gathered. The latest in multi-user technology is the Web

Object-Oriented environment, or **WOO**, where Web hypermedia capabilities are combined with MOO technology. These forms of real-time communication started out as ways of facilitating multi-user games; now they are being used to create virtual societies. For beginner information, see the Daedalus Group's page at <www.daedalus.com/net/border.html>.

A good place to get started with multi-user options is the Pueblo site at <www.chaco.com/pueblo/contents.html>. Pueblo is the client software needed to participate in virtual communities; this site also provides some general information and FAQs on multi-user communities.

Videoconferencing

Videoconferencing allows you and other people around the world who are signed on to the same conference, and who have the required audio and video software and hardware, to see and hear each other. You can also show each other images and text. One of the most popular software packages for video-conferencing is CU-SeeMe. For more information on videoconferencing, including CU-SeeMe and other software, go to <www.rocketcharged.com/cu-seeme/>.

File Transfer Protocol (FTP)

File transfer protocol (FTP) allows you to send or retrieve files from one computer to another. In reference to the Internet, it usually means downloading files (such as text files and software programs) from the Internet to your computer. You can download huge amounts of software for free or for a minimal charge at FTP archives, such as Shareware.com at <www.shareware.com>.

To download a file from an FTP archive, you need to log in with a user name and password. Most FTP archives use anonymous FTP, meaning that you use the word "anonymous" as your user name and your e-mail address as your password. Browsers equipped with FTP software will do this automatically, so that when you click on a file you want to download, it will begin downloading immediately.

The Internet provides a vast number of downloadable files, such as HTML editors (used for creating Web pages), chat software, graphics animators, games (including virtual reality), and screen savers. The easiest way to find these files is to go directly to a file archive, such as Shareware.com, where you can do a key word search, search the New Arrivals, or browse Most Popular Selections (the selections downloaded most often). Much of the software is free, called **freeware.** Some software, called **shareware,** requires a small fee. (Don't let Shareware.com's name fool you; most of its software is free!) In addition to Shareware.com, a good place to find software (as well as reviews and ratings of software) is ZDNet at <www5.zdnet.com>.

You can search for other FTP archives by using the search engine Archie, but Archie is not as user friendly as most of the search engines we have discussed so far. With Archie, you need to know the name of the software for which you are looking. There is also a Web-based interface for using Archie, called ArchiePlex at <www.nexor.com/public/archie/archieplex/archieplex.html>. Even though ArchiePlex is Web-based, it is still rather difficult to use, so read the instructions carefully before beginning any searches.

Most graphical Web browsers, such as Netscape and Explorer, come equipped with FTP software. However, this software is usually restricted to downloading files and is not capable of sending files. In order to send files, you need full-service FTP software, which you can download for free. For the Macintosh, you can get Fetch at <www.dartmouth.edu/pages/softdev/fetch.html>, or for a PC, you can get a free limited version of WS_FTP at <www.ipswitch.com/Downloads>.

Risks and Precautions

The following section deals with some of the risks that you may encounter while working with the Internet. We also suggest some precautions that may help you avoid some of the most common pitfalls.

Privacy

It is not a good idea to put anything in an e-mail message that you would not want others to see, because messages can be intercepted or sent to the wrong person. Especially if the computer you are using (or your receiver is using) belongs to your school or employer, your messages are very easy for others to access. There are privacy programs available, but using such a program may make people suspect that something secret is going on.

If you turn your computer into a server, you can have problems with individuals being able to access documents and information on your machine other than what you want to publish.

Personal Security

Sometimes you may be asked to give personal information on the Internet, especially when downloading commercial software. Reputable businesses have taken precautions to ensure the security of the information you provide. However, if you are unsure of the vendor or whenever you sign on to online news services, you should make a rule of giving just your first or last name and not giving your home address or phone number.

If you publish your own Web page (which will be discussed in Part Three), be aware that your page is accessible to the public. You want to give careful consideration to the personal information that you post on your page, such as your picture, phone numbers, and addresses. It is one thing for the whole world to have your e-mail address; it may be quite another for the whole world to be able to recognize you on sight and drive to where you live.

Copyright

It is safe to assume that most of the material on the Internet is copyrighted. The absence of a copyright notice does not mean that the material is not protected nor that it can be assumed to be in the public domain and therefore usable without seeking permission from the author or copyright holder. (For posting on the Web, however, the recommended procedure is to put "Copyright," the copyright symbol [©], the date published, the owner's name, and "All rights reserved" on documents that fall under copyright protection.) The only exception to using material from print sources that is protected by a copyright is *fair use*, which usually means reproduction of a limited amount of material for educational purposes, criticism, comment, or news reporting. However, fair use has not yet been extended to electronic media. For more information on copyright issues, see <lcweb.loc.gov/copyright>.

Ideas, facts, titles, names, short phrases, and blank forms are not protected by copyright. Items in the public domain, such as government documents or items for which copyright has expired, are not protected by copyright and may be used without permission.

Libel

When someone knowingly spreads false information about another person, harming that person's reputation, or defaming them, it is called slander. However, when such information is published in print, it is defamatory writing and may be considered libelous. The same caution applies to writing published on the Web, so make sure that any information you post is true and verifiable. Libel is a crime and is punishable as a felony.

Plagiarism

For Web documents, you can create a link to someone's Web page, but you may not cut and paste any part of someone's Web page and place it on your own. Similarly, if you quote Web-page information in a written document, you must cite it properly. (See the section on documentation, starting on page 14.)

Viruses

Viruses can be devastating to your computer. They can damage or destroy both hardware and software. Viruses can get into your computer in several ways. One way is to put an infected disk into your computer's disk drive and open a file on it. Viruses can also be downloaded from the Internet when you transfer files to your computer—for example, by downloading software or text files. Viruses can also be sent via e-mail: Reading a message is not generally a problem, but if you open an attachment contaminated with a virus, your computer will become infected. Basically, if you do anything with e-mail beyond reading the message itself, your computer is susceptible to viruses.

You can detect viruses and even prevent them from contaminating your computer with virus protection software. Some computers come with anti-virus software, but you can also purchase software or download it from the Internet. For the latest on computer viruses and anti-virus software, visit the Virus Bulletin Home Page at <www.virusbtn.com/Welcome.html>. There you will find information such as virus names, reviews of anti-virus software, and which viruses are currently at large.

PART THREE
FINDING JOBS ON THE INTERNET

When you start looking for jobs, whether full-time, part-time, or internships, the Internet has searchable databases of job postings by employers worldwide. This use of the Internet is one of its fastest growing areas and one which is especially important for students. Depending on the kind of job you are looking for, you can search by type of job, key word, or your skills and by city, state, or country.

Sites to Search for Jobs

With services like The Career Search Launch Pad at <www.pantos.org/cslp>, you can access several job-search engines. The Web pages available from the Launch Pad are Career Mosaic, NCS Career Magazine, NationJob, Online Career Center, and Net-Temps. You can access these career-search engines directly from the Launch Pad Web page, or you can link directly to each of them, using the URLs given below.

Career Mosaic <www.careermosaic.com>
Career Mosaic allows you to search for jobs on either the Web or Usenet by any one or any combination of

Skills description

Job title

Company name

City

State/Province

Country

Career Mosaic will sort job listings by most relevant jobs (best matches) or by most recent jobs. It will also help you get more information on top companies (browse company profiles), alert you to online job fairs, and give you access to success stories (letters from people who have used Career Mosaic). The site also includes tips on job hunting, résumé writing, and wage and salary information. Additionally, jobs can find you if you post your résumé on ResumeCM.

NationJob <www.nationjob.com>
NationJob allows you to search for jobs by any one or a combination of

Field (e.g., general business, engineering)

Location by U.S. region

Education (e.g., high school, bachelor's)

Job duration (full-time, part-time, temporary, or seasonal)

Salary

Key word search

Personal Job (P. J.) Scout is free and will help you search for a job; it will keep looking for jobs for you and e-mail updates on jobs that fit your qualifications. NationJob will help you get more information on companies (browse by field), find specialty job pages (browse available jobs by field), and let you read "Thank you PJ!" (success stories about using NationJob P. J.).

Online Career Center <www.occ.com>
Online Career Center allows you to search for jobs on the Web by any one or a combination of

Key words

City

State

With Online Career Center, you can get more information on member companies (possible employers), companies by category (industry, firms/agencies, contract, franchises), résumé writing, general career advice, corporate college recruiting, and colleges and universities.

Job Seeker Agent is free and will search for jobs for you. Each time you log on to your account, the latest jobs fitting your qualifications will be listed. Jobs can find you if you post your résumé onto OCC.

Net-Temps <www.net-temps.com>
Net-Temps allows you to search for jobs on the Web by any one or a combination of

Key words

State

USA

Net-Temps will help you get more information on employers as well. If you post your résumé to Net-Temps (you can post to the whole database or to a particular state), then jobs can also find you.

⌐🖰 **Info Bit**—As you can see, many of the job-finding services allow you to post your own résumé in their databank, which can make it easier for employers who are looking for someone with your unique blend of education and experiences. Usually, for you to post your résumé you will need to have a version written in hypertext markup language (HTML). The following section (pages 36–38) on creating your own Web page will get you off to a good start in creating an HTML version of your résumé.

Internships

A great place to start looking for internships is Yahoo!'s Internships category at <search.yahoo.com/bin/search?p=internships>. Some of the listings are as follows:

- Anchorage Animal Hospital
  www.alaska.net/~animhosp

- Campus International
  www.internship.de/

- Center for Photography at Woodstock
  www.cpw.org

- Construction Technology for Women
  www.contech.wittnn.com

- Environmental Careers Organization
  www.eco.org

- Explorations in Travel
  www.exploretravel.com

- Fund for American Studies
  www.dcinternships.org

- The Higher Education MoneyBook for Minorities and Women
  www.moneybook.com

- Independent Movie Production Jobs & Internships
  members.aol.com/crewjobs/

- Institute for Central American Development Studies
  www.icadscr.com

- International Educational Resource Center
  www.studyabroadierc.com

- JobSource
  www.jobsource.com

- Multicultural Alliance
  www.branson.org/mca

- Rising Star Internships
  www.rsinternships.com

- Tripod's National Internship Directory
  www.tripod.com/jobs_career/intern_visa
- Washington Center for Internships and Academic Seminars
  www.twc.edu
- WISE—Worldwide Internships & Service Education
  www.pitt.edu/~wise
- You and the Smithsonian
  www.si.edu/youandsi/start.htm

Scholarships

To find scholarship opportunities, go to Yahoo!'s scholarship site at <search.yahoo.com/search?p=scholarships>. Some of the listings are as follows:

- ExPAN Scholarship Search
  www.collegeboard.org/fundfinder/bin/fundfind01.pl
- fastWEB Financial Aid Search
  www.fastweb.com
- Rotary Foundation Ambassadorial Scholarships
  www.rotary.org/foundation/educational_programs
- Scholarships, Grants, & Financial Aid
  scholarship.vweb.net
- Scholarships for Women and Minorities
  members.aol.com/ox13qr/webpages/eyfswm1.html

Creating Your Own Web Pages

To post your own Web pages, you first need to make sure that your ISP has the ability to house them. There is usually an extra fee to store Web pages, so check to see what the rates are. Once you have a place to store your pages, the next step is to learn hypertext markup language (HTML). HTML uses **tags** contained in angle brackets, < >, to mark up the text of your document. Basically, HTML tags act as a set of instructions for the Web browser (such as Netscape); the tags tell the browser how your Web page should look (what's bold; what's in color; where pictures go), and how to respond to mouse clicks and keyboard strokes (if someone clicks on a link, where the browser should take them, or what Web page or file you are linking to). If you are not familiar with HTML, there is an excellent tutorial (created by Eric Meyer for Case Western University) called "Introduction to HTML." It can be found at <www.cwru.edu/help/introHTML/toc.html>. Also, after you start working with HTML, it's a good idea to have a cheat sheet with all the HTML tags. For such a list, go to the Bare Bones Guide for HTML 3.2 (or the most current version to date) by Kevin Werbach at <werbach.com/barebones/barebone.html>.

After learning the basics of HTML, you can begin posting Web pages. However, you may want to refer to some style guides for creating Web pages before you begin:

- Composing Good HTML
  www.cs.cmu.edu/~tilt/cgh
- Elements of HTML Style (a takeoff on Strunk & White)
  www.book.uci.edu/Staff/StyleGuide.html
- Style Guide for Online Hypertext
  www.w3.org/Provider/Style/Overview.html
- Sun Microsystems's Guide to Web Style
  www.sun.com/styleguide
- Web Etiquette Guide
  www.w3.org/Provider/Style/Etiquette.html

Once you start posting Web pages, there are several key points that you should remember:

For text—

- Link to your e-mail address.
- Include a "last updated" date.
- Format text for readability.
- Do not leave any dead ends—always include a link back to your home page.
- Annotate any lists of links you include.
- Include a "Back to Top" link for long pages.

For images—

- Help minimize download time by creating small image files (**GIF** or **JPEG**).
- Use alternative text for images in case someone has disabled Auto Load Images.
- Use text links in addition to links on image maps (pictures with inserted links).

Be sure to check your page on different machines and on different browsers to make sure that it looks the way you want it to. Also, remember that the information you are posting is available to anyone, so be careful what kind of personal information you post, such as pictures, phone numbers, and addresses (see "Personal Security," page 30).

Once you have your Web pages ready for the rest of the world, the final step is to make them available through search engines (such as Yahoo! or AltaVista).

For other people to be able to look up your page with a search engine, you have to submit it. Of course it would be quite time-consuming to submit your page to each search engine. To help make this task easier, there is a free service called Submit It! at <www.submit-it.com>. Have fun!

PART FOUR
INTERNET RESOURCES

Change is inherent in the Web. As we prepared this guide, we verified every URL we listed. But by the time you read it, some of them are bound to have changed. If you follow one of our URLs and receive an error message, try typing the title of the document into your favorite search engine (such as Yahoo! or AltaVista). On the Web good things hardly ever disappear, although they do move around a lot. (Be advised that some of these services charge a user or subscription fee.) Be sure to check Part Five for specific resources in anthropology.

Reference Material
Dictionaries and Thesauruses
- Oxford English Dictionary
  www.oed.com
- Roget's Thesaurus (version 1.02)
  www.thesaurus.com
- Webster's Revised Unabridged Dictionary, 1913 edition
  humanities.uchicago.edu/forms_unrest/webster.form.html
- Various dictionaries and thesauruses
  www.dictionary.com

Citations and Copyright
- Citation Styles for Electronic Media
  lamp.infosys.utas.edu.au/citation.html
- Council of Biology Editors
  www.cbe.org/CBE
- Electronic Sources: APA Style of Citation
  www.uvm.edu/~xli/reference/apa.html
- A Guide for Writing Research Papers Based on Modern Language Association (MLA) Documentation
  155.43.225.30/mla.html
- IEEE
  www.ieee.org
- Research and Writing Guides
  library.scar.utoronto.ca/Bladen_Library/ResearchWritingGuides.html
- U.S. Copyright Office Home Page
  lcweb.loc.gov/copyright

- Writing Center: Chicago Style (by the University of Wisconsin–Madison)
  www.wisc.edu/writing/Handbook/DocChicago.html

Quotations
- Bartlett's Quotations (1901 edition)
  www.columbia.edu/acis/bartleby/bartlett
- The Quotations Page
  www.starlingtech.com/quotes

Libraries
- Internet Public Library
  ipl.sils.umich.edu
- Library of Congress
  lcweb.loc.gov/catalog/booksquery.html

News and Media

Print
- Atlantic Unbound (*The Atlantic Monthly*)
  www.theatlantic.com/atlantic/coverj.htm
- The *New York Times*
  www.nytimes.com
- *San Jose Mercury News*
  www.sjmercury.com
- *Time*
  pathfinder.com/time
- *USA Today*
  www.usatoday.com

Broadcast
- CNN
  www.cnn.com
- MSNBC
  www.msnbc.com
- National Public Radio
  www.npr.org
- PBS
  www.pbs.org
- WIRED News
  www.wired.com

News Filters
- Pointcast (news filter/screen saver)
  www.pointcast.com
- CRAYON
  crayon.net

Books and Book Reviews
- Amazon.com
  www.amazon.com
- BookWire (*Publishers Weekly* Web page, including best-seller lists)
  www.bookwire.com
- Borders on the Web
  www.borders.com
- Dial-A-Book Chapter One
  www1.psi.net/chapterone
- The Independent Reader (leading booksellers' recommendations)
  www.independentreader.com
- Salon Magazine
  www.salonmagazine.com

Online Writing Centers
- The Alliance for Computers and Writing (Comprehensive—the only one you'll really need.)
  english.ttu.edu/acw/acw.html
- A Guide for Writing Research Papers (Excellent interactive grammar tutorials.)
  155.43.225.30/mla.htm
- Paradigm Online Writing Assistant
  www.idbsu.edu/english/cguilfor/paradigm

People Finders
- BigFoot
  www.bigfoot.com
- Four11
  www.four11.com
- InfoSpace
  www.infospace.com

- Netscape's White Pages (Community building)
  home.netscape.com/escapes/whitepages/community.html
- Switchboard
  www.switchboard.com
- WhoWhere?
  www.whowhere.com

Cool Stuff

- c|net (A Web surfing must—something for everyone.)
  www.cnet.com
- The Discovery Channel
  www.discovery.com
- IPIX (Download IPIX's immersive image plugin and take virtual tours of places like the space shuttle and Chicago's Field Museum.)
  www.ipix.com
- MTV (Most everything from videos to music news.)
  www.mtv.com
- Mag's Big List of HTML Editors (If you know HTML and wish you had an editor to help, this list will have something for you.)
  www.davis.k12.ut.us/knowlton/LDSBC/webclass/editors.htm
- Mapquest (Find places, plan the routes for your trips, and don't forget to try the interactive world atlas.)
  www.mapquest.com/
- Megabyte University Discussion List (Find out more about MUDs, MOOs, etc.)
  www.daedalus.com/MBU/MBU.intro.html
- Netscape Plug-ins (Browse the different and mostly free components that you can download and add to your Netscape browser, such as audio, video, and animation software.)
  home.netscape.com/comprod/mirror/navcomponents_download.html
- The Virtual Library of Museums (Browse museums by country, by exhibition, or by special interest; even contains virtual tours.)
  www.comlab.ox.ac.uk/archive/other/museums.html
- Yahoo!'s Games (Yahoo!'s directory of fun and games.)
  www.yahoo.com/Recreation/Games

Sites for Teachers

- Editor & Publisher Home Page
  www.mediainfo.com
- The National Writing Centers Association Page
  departments.colgate.edu/diw/NWCA/WCResources.html
- THE SLOT: A Spot for Copy Editors
  www.theslot.com
- Workshops for Copy Editors in Book and Magazine Publishing
  www.copyeditor.com/BookMagazineWorkshops.html
- World Lecture Hall
  www.utexas.edu/world/lecture
- Writing Across the Curriculum Guide (Bibliography)
  orchard.cortland.edu/WACguide/WACsection2.html

Newsgroups

Newsgroups have specific notations for different kinds of discussion groups to help in organizing Usenet's hierarchical structure. These categories are the following:

alt	alternative newsgroups
bionet	biology
biz	business
ClariNet	news feeds
comp	computers
k12	education
misc	miscellaneous
news	Usenet info
rec	hobbies, sports
sci	general science
soc	social topics
talk	anything

Some Newsgroups for Students

- alt.education.student.government
- alt.humor.best-of-usenet
- alt.journalism.students
- rec.music.makers.songwriting
- soc.college.gradinfo

Some Newsgroups for Teachers

- alt.books.reviews
- alt.education
- misc.writing

PART FIVE
ANTHROPOLOGY ON THE INTERNET

This guide is not intended to be a thorough coverage of anthropological materials available on the Internet. There are far too many of these—especially if one includes sites in all languages—to be mentioned in totality. Furthermore, the Internet is constantly changing, with new discussion groups, Web sites, and other resources being added and modified on a daily basis. What is there today may not be there tomorrow. However, it is certain that the content of anthropology on the Internet is expanding at a breathtaking rate. At the time this guide was written, a search on "anthropology" by AltaVista listed over 700,000 individual Web pages. To get an idea of what this means, if it were possible to spend twelve hours a day browsing the Web at the rate of one document a minute, it would take over two years just to *glance* at each page! Given the likely prospect that the amount of digitized information will increase exponentially over time, it is critical that students develop basic skills for finding what is available and how much of it is useful to them. It is important to think of this guide as a starting point for exploration of basic resources of interest to anthropologists on the Internet. It will have served its purpose if it persuades you to take a drive on the information superhighway. Where you go and what you learn on your journey is entirely up to you.

Finding Anthropology on the Internet

Search Engines
Perhaps the most important tools for finding anthropology on the Internet are search engines, computer programs that organize and provide access to huge quantities of information. Among the best search engines currently available are the following:

- AltaVista
  www.altavista.digital.com
- Excite
  www.excite.com
- Infoseek
  www.infoseek.com
- Lycos
  www.lycos.com
- Metacrawler (A service that searches several of these other search engines at a time, providing comprehensive—if somewhat slower—searches.)
  www.metacrawler.com

- WebCrawler
  www.webcrawler.com

All of these search engines provide methods of complex searching, in which one can look for phrases and include Boolean operators (AND, OR, NOT, NEAR, etc.). They also allow for searches of both the World Wide Web and Usenet. Given the enormous number of documents available, it is best to search for words and phrases that will be specifically relevant to what you are seeking. AltaVista now has features that will allow users to include or exclude a variety of potential key words, helping to narrow a search considerably. It also provides a basic language translator for reading Web pages in languages other than English.

Finding Out About Anthropology Programs and Anthropologists

Undergraduate and Graduate Programs. It has become quite common for anthropology departments at major colleges and universities to establish a presence on the Internet, especially in the form of home pages on the World Wide Web. Department home pages can be excellent sources of information. Most provide information about the strengths of a department and the nature of its programs. Many contain rosters of faculty with descriptions of their specific research interests and current projects. Some will even offer access to information about specific courses, field schools, and employment opportunities.

One of the best directories of anthropology department home pages is provided by Yahoo! <www.yahoo.com> in a section of their Social Science directory <www.yahoo.com/Social_Science/Anthropology_and_Archaeology/Institutes/College_and_University_Departments>.

E-mail Addresses of Anthropologists. The widespread use of e-mail has made it possible to quickly and easily contact most individuals who are associated with colleges and universities as well as people who work for nonacademic organizations. Hugh Jarvis at the State University of New York–Buffalo has compiled a worldwide directory of e-mail addresses for anthropologists that is available on the Web:

- Worldwide E-mail Directory of Anthropologists (Provides access to basic information on how to contact over 3000 individuals at over 1000 different institutions.)
  wings.buffalo.edu/academic/department/anthropology/weda

While many anthropologists are accustomed to receiving e-mail from strangers, you should be careful not to abuse the ease with which they can be contacted. Considerate requests for information are not inappropriate, however, and often the best way to find information is to go directly to one of the experts in the field. As a general rule, it is best to keep e-mail contacts brief and to the point. Don't forget that the person to whom you are writing may be receiving *many* other messages similar to yours.

Online Discussions

Usenet

Usenet is a Unix-based information system that maintains thousands of special-interest discussion groups called newsgroups. Access to Usenet is provided through university computing accounts and other Internet service providers (ISPs). You should seek more information locally if you do not know how to access these resources.

Usenet newsgroup discussions differ from listservs in that messages are not sent directly to individual users, but stored on servers from which they can be retrieved. Usenet newsgroups tend to be used by a much wider audience than individual listservs. The topics of messages can be extremely varied, and the tone of the discussions is often quite heated. Messages that are deemed silly, confrontational, or offensive are likely to be flamed by a flurry of irate responses. Be forewarned: Newsgroups are not for the faint of heart! Most of the Usenet newsgroups are not moderated, meaning that no one is exercising control over the quantity or quality of messages being posted. As a result, the archaeology groups tend to be dominated by discussions of alternative, nonacademic, or pseudoscientific theories of the kind addressed in Kenneth Feder's book *Frauds, Myths, and Mysteries*. Similarly, physical anthropology discussions tend to be laden with debates between creationists and scientists about the theory of evolution. If you need help with critical thinking, an excellent resource on the Web is

- *The Skeptic's Dictionary* (Online book that provides a critical analysis of dozens of topics that merit a skeptical consideration.) wheel.ucdavis.edu/%7Ebtcarrol/skeptic/dictcont.html

Alternatively, you may want to stick with the moderated discussions, in which at least one individual reads and judges the merits of messages before they are posted to the list. The following is a list of current Usenet newsgroups offered by most providers and the subjects on which they entertain discussions:

- alt.archaeology—Archaeology
- alt.culture.*—Discussions of individual cultures (there are over 70 subgroups)
- alt.history.ancient-worlds—Ancient world history
- alt.native—Native American issues (superceded by soc.culture.native)
- sci.anthropology—Anthropology
- sci.anthropology.paleo—Evolution of humans and other primates
- sci.archaeology—Archaeology
- sci.archaeology.moderated—Archaeology (moderated)
- sci.archaeology.mesoamerican—Archaeology of Mexico and Central America
- sci.lang—Linguistics

- soc.culture.*—Discussions of individual cultures (there are over 150 subgroups)
- soc.culture.native—Native American issues
- soc.history.ancient—Ancient history
- soc.misc—Social issues
- soc.religion.*—Discussions of world religions (there are over 15 subgroups)
- talk.origins—Human origins and the theory of evolution

Listservs

Listservs are programs running on Internet servers that allow for the management of lists of e-mail addresses. These programs will receive messages sent to the listserv's e-mail address and then immediately redistribute copies of that message to other addresses on the list. The effect is to create an electronic bulletin board on which messages can be posted and read by hundreds of users. Some lists can have thousands of members; others will have only a dozen or so. Members can respond to messages either publicly (on the list) or privately (through a direct e-mail message). "Traffic," or the rate at which new messages appear on the listserv, can range from one message a week to dozens in a single day. Listservs differ substantially from most Usenet newsgroups in that they are controlled by a "listowner," who has the ability to control access to subscriptions and monitor messages before they are posted and even has the power to delete any subscriber from the list. Listserv discussions tend to be much more professional than Usenet newsgroups. Most have open subscriptions, but some are highly exclusive, allowing subscriptions only from individuals with specific qualifications. It is always advisable to read all the instructions and guidelines for the use of a specific list before posting a message.

On a well-maintained list, all messages should be clearly labeled. Some e-mail programs, such as Netscape Mail, Pegasus Mail, and Eudora Pro, will display messages with the same "Subject" line together as a thread, permitting you to read contributions to a discussion that may stretch over several days or weeks.

Some lists have advanced features that permit subscribers to specify the categories of messages they would like to receive. Frivolous posts and requests that look as if you are trying to get someone else to do your homework are likely to be flamed with negative, mocking, or even insulting responses. Some lists are moderated by an individual or a panel in an attempt to eliminate silly, useless, distracting, off-topic, or offensive messages. Most lists encourage new subscribers to lurk (read messages without posting) in order to familiarize themselves with the level and kind of discussion before generating new e-mail with contributions to the list. Try to get an idea of the kinds of participants and their personalities before jumping into a discussion. If you are considering submitting a message to a listserv, don't forget that copies of it will go out to hundreds, if not thousands, of potential professors, colleagues, and employers. As one listowner writes, "It is better to remain silent and be thought a fool than to post a message and remove all doubt." Many lists archive their messages and make them available on the Web. While this has clear benefits, it also means that messages may become part of a searchable database that is available for many years.

One of the most valuable functions of a listserv is to allow you to ask a question to hundreds of "experts" at the same time, some of whom are likely to respond with helpful information and may want to develop professional relationships. In general, it is not a good idea to draw off too much information without providing something useful in return. The community of the Internet runs mostly on reciprocity—the willingness of participants to contribute in return for what they use. Common methods of reciprocation include posting bibliographic references, book reviews, information about new Web sites, summaries of news reports, or even creating your own Web resources to help fill in gaps that exist in the growing body of online information.

The most common way to subscribe is to send the following e-mail message to the address of the listserv:

```
subscribe [list name] [your name]
```

Upon subscribing, you will receive an information message describing the purpose of the listserv and the rules for participation.

The following are just a few of the dozens of anthropology-related listservs on the Internet. For a more complete listing with specific subscription rules, see the relevant section of Allen Lutins's Anthropology Resources on the Internet <www.nitehawk.com/alleycat/anth-faq.html>.

- AIA-L (Moderated list on archaeology and ancient technology.)
  majordomo@brynmawr.edu

- ANTHEORY-L (Anthropological theory.)
  listserv@list.nih.gov

- ANTHRO-L (General discussion list for anthropology. The ANTHRO-L WWW site is located at <www.anatomy.su.oz.au/danny/anthropology/anthro-l>, with additional archives at <listserv.acsu.buffalo.edu/archives/anthro-l.html>.)
  listserv@ubvm.cc.buffalo.edu

- ARCHAEO-L (Discussion list for beginning students of archaeology.)
  listproc@ukans.edu

- ARCHCOMP-L (Archaeological computing.)
  listserv@listserv.acsu.buffalo.edu

- ARCH-L (General discussion list for archaeology. The ARCH-L archives are available on the Web at <listserv.tamu.edu/archives/arch-l.html>.)
  listserv@tamvm1.tamu.edu

- ARCH-STUDENT (Discussion list for students of archaeology.)
  listproc@lists.colorado.edu

- AZTLAN (Pre-Columbian studies.)
  listserv@ulkyvm.louisville.edu
- DEVEL-L (Issues in international development.)
  listserv@american.edu
- ETHMUS-L (Discussion list for ethnomusicology.)
  listserv@umdd.umd.edu
- ETHNOHIS (Ethnology, history, and ethnohistory.)
  listserv@hearn.nic.surfnet.nl
- HISTARCH (Historical archaeology.)
  listserv@asuvm.inre.asu.edu
- INTERCUL (Intercultural communication.)
  comserve@vm.ecs.rpi.edu
- LANGUAGE-CULTURE (Linguistic anthropology.)
  language-culture-request@cs.uchicago.edu
- LINGANTH (Linguistic anthropology.)
  Linganth-Request@cc.rochester.edu
- LINGUIST (Linguistics, with discussions archived at <www.emich.edu/
  ~linguist>.)
  listserv@tamvm1.tamu.edu
- LITHICS-L (Archaeological lithic analysis.)
  listserv@acsu.buffalo.edu
- MUSEUM-L (Museum issues.)
  listserv@unmvma.unm.edu
- PALEOANTHRO (Paleoanthropology.)
  Majordomo@list.pitt.edu
- PAN-L (General discussion list for physical anthropology.)
  listserv@psuorvm.cc.pdx.edu
- PRIMATOLOGY (Primates, both human and nonhuman.)
  mailbase@mailbase.ac.uk
- SBANTH-L (Anthropology graduate students.)
  listserv@ucsbvm.ucsb.edu
- SPANBORD (History and archaeology of the Spanish borderlands region.)
  listserv@asuvm.inre.asu.edu
- WOMANTH-L (Women in anthropology.)
  listserv@relay.doit.wisc.edu
- XCULT-X (Cross-cultural communication.)
  listserv@psuvm.psu.edu

World Wide Web Resources

General Information and Links

There are several excellent index home pages on the Web that provide many links to anthropology resources on the Internet. While many of them refer to the same sites, each is maintained and updated by a different individual at a different institution. Some sites will provide the date of the last update, which will give you a good idea of whether the site has links to the most recent additions to the Web. Depending on the activity level of the Webmaster, some sites may sit unattended for months. For this reason, it is a good idea to look at several different index sites and to visit each one more than once over a period of time.

Most Web browsers permit you to create personal lists of URLs that are stored on your own computer. Known as bookmarks or favorites, these files are ones that you can update quickly and easily. It is a good practice to mark pages that you find useful as you surf the Web. There are few things more frustrating than trying to find a Web site again when you have forgotten the series of links that got you there in the first place! Browser software also will allow you to assign your own names to or record personal notes about individual links.

Be aware that a common problem with hypertext pages linked to external resources (especially true for index pages) is a condition known as "link rot." This occurs when changes are made to the URLs of individual linked pages, often as a result of changes in domain names or directory structures, without changes being made in the links that point to them. In these cases, bad links produce only error messages. If you encounter a bad link, it is good netiquette to send a brief message to the person who maintains the page on which it is found. This will help them to find and (hopefully) fix the link for future visitors. A valuable (and free!) service that will keep you informed about changes to specific Web sites is NetMind <www.netmind.com>, where you can register to be notified via e-mail when your favorite sites are updated.

The following are some of the best Web sites for finding links to other resources:

- AnthroLink (Site dedicated to material for instructors in secondary schools and community colleges. Offers message board, links, and other materials.) www.buckley.pvt.k12.ca.us/AnthroLink

- AnthroNet (A resource at the University of Virginia.) www.people.Virginia.EDU/~dew7e/anthronet

- Anthropological Multimedia (An experiment in multiple-authored online documents.) www.rsl.ox.ac.uk/isca/marcus.banks.02.html

- Anthropology Communications On-Line pegasus.acs.ttu.edu/~wurlr/anthro.html

- Anthropology in the News (Links to news stories that are accessible on the Web.)
  www.tamu.edu/anthropology/news.html
- Anthropology Resources on the Internet (Maintained by Allen "Alleycat" Lutins. This is one of the most comprehensive sources of information on Usenet newsgroups, listservs, and Web pages available on the Internet. Because it provides URLs in both hypertext and regular text, it can be readily downloaded and printed for use in hardcopy form.)
  www.nitehawk.com/alleycat/anth-faq.html
- Anthropology Web Sites (A list maintained by John Kantner for the Deptartment of Anthropology at the University of California–Santa Barbara.)
  www.anth.ucsb.edu/netinfo.html
- Cyberspace Culture and Society (Collection of materials related to the culture of cyberspace.)
  umbc7.umbc.edu/~curnoles/cybersoc.html
- LSU Libraries Webliography: Anthropology (A regularly updated index of Web sites about anthropology.)
  www.lib.lsu.edu/soc/anthro.html
- Matt's Paleo Pages (Award-winning suite of resources for paleoanthropology, archaeology, and other ancient concerns—including dinosaurs. Created and maintained by Matt Fraser.)
  www.pitt.edu/~mattf/PaleoPage.html
- Nicole's AnthroPage (A student-maintained list with lots of useful links.)
  www.wsu.edu:8000/~i9248809/anthrop.html
- Suite 101–Anthropology (An intelligent index with links to topic discussions, managed by Anita Cohen-Williams.)
  www.suite101.com/topics/page.cfm/234
- University of Arizona Library: Anthropology and Archaeology on the Internet
  dizzy.library.arizona.edu/users/jlcox/first.html
- University of Buffalo Anthropology: Direct Access to Web Anthropology Resources
  wings.buffalo.edu/academic/department/anthropology/web_sites
- Virtual Library: Anthropology (List of links categorized by subject.)
  anthrotech.com/resources
- Web Site Excellence–Anthropology (Links to sites judged to be among the best on the Web for dissemination of information about anthropology.)
  anthro.org/fourstar.htm
- Western Connecticut State University List: Anthropology Internet Resources
  www.wcsu.ctstateu.edu/socialsci/antres.html

- Yahoo! (Ever-growing list of links provided by Yahoo!, one of the first and most comprehensive indexes of the Web.)
  www.yahoo.com/Social_Science/Anthropology_and_Archaeology
- Yahoo:Regional:Countries (The ability to visit the far corners of the globe with just a few clicks of the mouse is here.)
  www.yahoo.com/Regional/Countries

Online Aids to Library Research

While most people use the Web to find online resources, there are many Web sites that have been created to facilitate library research using traditional print media. These include bibliographic databases, online catalogues, and descriptions of a wide variety of library materials. If the information you are seeking is not available on the Web, you may be able to find it in the library. It is unlikely that *all* of the library material relevant to anthropological research will ever be completely digitized. Given that the vast majority of anthropological literature exists only in print publications, these online aids are critical for any thorough research project.

- Anita's Bookshelf: Anthropology/Archaeology Books (New books in anthropology, selected by Anita Cohen-Williams.)
  www.angelfire.com/ca/cohwill
- Anthropological Index Online (Searchable database for bibliographic records between 1965 and 1993.)
  lucy.ukc.ac.uk/AIO.html
- Anthropology Branch of the Smithsonian Institution Libraries (An excellent source for a wide variety of information. Unfortunately, many of the links to online resources have restricted access.)
  www.sil.si.edu/Branches/anth-hp.htm
- Anthropology: Some Potentially Useful Reference Sources (From Regenstein Library, University of Chicago.)
  www.lib.uchicago.edu/LibInfo/SourcesBySubject/Anthropology/antref.html
- ARD–The Anthropology Review Database (ARD) (Searchable database of online reviews of anthropological resources ranging from books and articles to Web sites and CD-ROMs.)
  wings.buffalo.edu/ARD
- Handbook of Latin American Studies (Database of all volumes of this major reference, accessible through a powerful search engine.)
  lcweb2.loc.gov/hlas
- Human Relations Area Files (HRAF) (Database of cultural information, based at Yale University and available in one format or another at most major university libraries.)
  www.yale.edu/hraf/home.htm

- Resources in Anthropology (Compiled by Brita Servaes, Milton S. Eisenhower Library, The Johns Hopkins University.)
  milton.mse.jhu.edu:8001/research/anthropology/anthropology.html
- Selected Resources in Anthropology (Compiled by Nancy S. Skipper at Cornell University.)
  www.library.cornell.edu/okuref/anthrweb.htm

Online Course Materials

An increasing number of faculty at institutions around the world are using the Web as a way to provide students with materials relevant to college-level courses. The quantity and quality of these materials will only increase over time. The following URLs, together with those listed below for the various subfields of anthropology, will give you ideas and models for how one might use Web resources as a teaching tool. If you are a student in an anthropology course, these sites provide excellent ways to supplement (or double-check) your own notes.

- Archaeology and Anthropology (A collection of essays and papers by Mike Shupp.)
  www.csun.edu/~ms44278/anthro.htm
- A History of Anthropology (Course home page for a graduate seminar at the University of Kansas.)
  www.ukans.edu/~hoopes/701
- *Human Antiquity* Update (Electronic "newsletter" with updates to *Human Antiquity: An Introduction to Physical Anthropology and Archaeology,* by Kenneth L. Feder and Michael Alan Park.)
  www.anthropology.ccsu.edu/human_antiquity/update.html
- Into the World of Anthropology (An excellent resource for the four-field approach, created and maintained by Bonnie Sklar at the University of Illinois–Champaign/Urbana.)
  lrs.ed.uiuc.edu/students/b-sklar/basic387.html
- Introduction to Anthropology (ANTH 106) (Taught by Nicholas Bellantoni at the University of Connecticut. Beautiful and effective design. Includes automatically graded practice tests.)
  spirit.lib.uconn.edu/ArchNet/Topical/Educat/anth106/spring96/anth96.html

Anthropology Museums

Most major anthropology museums, as well as museums with larger missions but substantial holdings in anthropology, have developed Web sites to facilitate communication with scholars and the general public. Museum Web sites contain basic information about the museums and their collections. Some offer special online exhibitions. Several even offer searchable collections databases.

- ArchNet: Museums on the Web (General index of links to museums that house anthropological materials and exhibitions, with codes indicating principal strengths.)
  spirit.lib.uconn.edu/ArchNet/Museums/Museums.html

- Florida Museum of Natural History (Known for its excellent collections of material from Florida and the Caribbean.)
  www.flmnh.ufl.edu

- Mankato State University EMuseum (An excellent example of a "virtual" anthropology museum.)
  www.anthro.mankato.msus.edu

- Peabody Museum of Archaeology and Ethnology (Web site at Harvard University that features online exhibitions and indices of archival material.)
  www.peabody.harvard.edu

- Peabody Museum of Natural History (Features a searchable catalogue of artifacts, complete with images.)
  www.peabody.yale.edu

- Phoebe Hearst Museum (UC Berkeley) (Formerly the Lowie Museum, this is one of the oldest and finest anthropology museums in the United States.)
  www.qal.berkeley.edu/~hearst

- Royal Ontario Museum (This Toronto museum has rich archaeological and ethnographic collections.)
  www.rom.on.ca

- Smithsonian Institution (The first major collection of anthropological material in the United States, together with a lot of other fascinating collections.)
  www.si.edu

- University of Michigan Museum of Anthropology (An excellent resource in Ann Arbor.)
  www.umma.lsa.umich.edu

- University Museum, University of Pennsylvania (Another great museum site, with online exhibitions and abundant information.)
  www.upenn.edu/museum

Professional Societies
An increasing number of professional societies have created Web pages to provide information about their organizations. The following are just a few of the places to find out more about them:

- American Anthropological Association
  www.ameranthassn.org

- American Cultural Resources Association
  www.acra-crm.org

- Archaeological Institute of America
  www.archaeological.org
- Dental Anthropology Association
  www.sscf.ucsb.edu/~walker
- Federation of Small Anthropology Programs
  www.umd.umich.edu/~dmoerman/fosap.html
- National Association of State Archaeologists
  nasa.uconn.edu
- Society for American Archaeology
  www.saa.org
- Society for Applied Anthropology
  www.telepath.com/sfaa
- Society for Archaeological Sciences
  www.wisc.edu/larch/sas/sas.htm
- Society for Economic Anthropology
  www.agnesscott.edu/academic/ps_s_a/rees/sea/index.htm
- Society for Historic Archaeology
  www.azstarnet.com/~sha
- Society for Industrial Archeology
  www.ss.mtu.edu/IA/sia.html
- Society for Professional Archeologists
  www.smu.edu/~anthrop/sopa.html
- Society for Visual Anthropology
  www.xensei.com/docued/sva

Journals and Online Publications
The journals listed below do not (yet) offer online versions of the articles that
are published in them. However, most provide indexes to current and past
issues as well as additional information about the publications themselves. They
also provide guidelines and rules for submissions.

- *American Antiquity*
  www.saa.org/Publications/AmAntiq/amantiq.html
- *American Journal of Physical Anthropology*
  www.interscience.wiley.com/jpages/0002-9483
- *Andean Past*
  kramer.ume.maine.edu/~anthrop/AndeanP.html
- *Anthropology Today*
  lucy.ukc.ac.uk/rai/at.html

- *Antiquity*
  intarch.ac.uk/antiquity
- *Anthropoetics*
  www2.humnet.ucla.edu/humnet/anthropoetics/home.html
- *Anthropological Linguistics*
  www.indiana.edu/~anthling
- *Archaeology Magazine*
  www.he.net/~archaeol
- *Cultural Anthropology Methods (CAM)*
  www.lawrence.edu/~bradleyc/cam.html
- *Current Anthropology*
  www.artsci.wustl.edu/~anthro/ca
- *Current Archaeology*
  www.archaeology.co.uk
- *Evolutionary Anthropology*
  www.interscience.wiley.com/jpages/1060-1538
- *Journal of Anthropological Archaeology*
  www.apnet.com/www/journal/aa.htm
- *Journal of Archaeological Science*
  www.hbuk.co.uk/ap/journals/as
- *Journal of Field Archaeology*
  jfa-www.bu.edu
- *Journal of Human Evolution*
  www.hbuk.co.uk/ap/journals/hu.htm
- *Journal of Political Ecology*
  dizzy.library.arizona.edu/ej/jpe/jpeweb.html
- *Journal of World Anthropology*
  wings.buffalo.edu/academic/department/anthropology/jwa
- *Latin American Antiquity*
  www.saa.org/Publications/LatAmAnt/latamant.html
- *Population Index*
  popindex.princeton.edu
- *Theoretical Anthropology*
  www.univie.ac.at/voelkerkunde/theoretical-anthropology

The following electronic journals represent innovative uses of the Web for direct publication of anthropological and archaeological research. They do not have corresponding paper versions, but exist solely as electronic resources.

- *AZTLAN E-Journal* (Articles on pre-Columbian studies.)
  www.ukans.edu/~hoopes/aztlan
- *The Electronic Journal of Generative Anthropology*
  www.sil.si.edu/elecedns.htm
- *Internet Archaeology*
  intarch.york.ac.uk
- *Online Archaeology*
  avebury.arch.soton.ac.uk/Journal/journal.html

Physical/Biological Anthropology

Online Course Materials. As with other subareas of anthropology, there is a growing body of instructional material available on the Web. The following sites have been developed primarily for introductory-level students. They provide course outlines and a wide variety of both textual and visual materials.

- Anth 1101 Human Origins Website (Course taught at the University of Minnesota.)
  www.geocities.com/Athens/Acropolis/5579/TA.html
- Anthropology 233: Human Evolution (Course taught by Sally McBrearty at the University of Connecticut.)
  www.lib.uconn.edu/ArchNet/Topical/Educat/anth233/233-SYL.html
- ASM 101: Human Origins and Development of Culture (Course taught by Richard Effland at Mesa Community College.)
  www.mc.maricopa.edu/anthro/origins/asm97.html
- Human Origins and Evolution (Course taught by Jean Sept at Indiana University.)
  www.indiana.edu/~origins
- Humb 1060 The History of Man: Human Evolution (Course taught at the University of Leeds.)
  www.leeds.ac.uk/chb/h1060.html
- McGraw-Hill Anthropology Newsletters (Online news about physical anthropology.)
  www.mhhe.com/socscience/anthropology/newsletters.mhtml

Human Evolution. The evolution of humans is a topic of enormous interest on the Web. You will find resources that range from in-depth discussions of evolutionary theory to documentation of fossil hominids and late-breaking news about recent scientific discoveries.

- Australopithecine Sex Change (Brief discussion of sexing controversy from McGraw-Hill.)
  www.mhhe.com/socscience/anthropology/aspring96.html

- Enter Evolution: Theory and History (Resource on the intellectual history of evolutionary theory.)
www.ucmp.berkeley.edu/history/evolution.html
- The Evolution of Man Directory (General overview of human evolution by Shawn Donaldson.)
www.wf.carleton.ca/Museum/man/begin.html
- Fossil Hominids (Resource for online information about human ancestors and evolutionary theory. Part of the Talk.Origins Archive.)
www.talkorigins.org/faqs/fossil-hominids.html
- Hominid Evolution Bibliography (List of published sources on fossil hominids and human evolution.)
www.ipfw.indiana.edu/east1/coon/web/hominid.htm
- Institute of Human Origins (Home page of this nonprofit organization.)
www.asu.edu/clas/iho/
- Introduction to Biological Anthropology (Web site to support John Relethford's course at the State University of New York College at Oneonta, based on his textbook *The Human Species: An Introduction to Biological Anthropology*.)
www.oneonta.edu/~anthro/anth130
- Introduction to Primates (Information about primates and primatology.)
members.aol.com/PamNoble/primpage/homepage.html
- MendelWeb (Information about Gregor Mendel and Mendelian genetics.)
hermes.astro.washington.edu/mirrors/MendelWeb/MWtoc.html
- The Origins of Humankind (Comprehensive resource for the study of human evolution that provides images of fossils, bibliographies, discussions of new discoveries, and links to other Web resources.)
www.dealsonline.com/origins
- PaleoChat (Real-time interactive chat for discussions of topics in paleontology, paleoanthropology, archaeology, and evolutionary biology.)
www.pitt.edu/~mattf/PaleoChat.html
- Talk.Origins (Web site created by Jim Foley. Its principal focus is on educating the public about evolutionary theory, specifically as it applies to human beings. Includes detailed information about fossil hominids and FAQs about the theory of evolution. This page was developed to support discussions on the Talk.Origins Usenet newsgroup.)
www.talkorigins.org

Primate Studies. The following is just a sample of Web sites dealing with primatology. Information on specific species should be sought using the capabilities of individual search engines.

- African Primates at Home (Features general information and audio files of primate vocalizations.)
  www.indiana.edu/~primate/primates.html
- Dental Microwear Web Site (Presents the kinds of methods being used to study fossil primate eating habits.)
  comp.uark.edu/~pungar
- Primate Handedness and Brain Lateralization Research Site (Provides useful links to other primate sites.)
  www.indiana.edu/~primate
- Primate-Jobs (Site for individuals seeking employment opportunities in primatology.)
  www.primate.wisc.edu/pin/jobs

Human Genetics and Biological Diversity. Studies of human biological diversity and the composition of the human genome are generating a huge quantity of valuable information on the Web. The following are just a few of the sites that provide access to summaries of recent work. A number of researchers have developed software to assist with taxonomy and the mapping of phylogenetic trees. Many of these are readily available for download from the Web.

- Anthropometry Resource Center (Information on how to measure the human body.)
  www.odc.com/anthro
- Danish Centre for Human Genome Research
  biobase.dk/cgi-bin/celis
- Human Genome Databases Menu
  www.hgmp.mrc.ac.uk/GenomeWeb/human-gen-db.html>
- The Human Genome Diversity Project (Summary document.)
  www-leland.stanford.edu/group/morrinst/Alghero.html
- The Human Genome Project (Information on this research initiative.)
  www.ncgr.org/ncgr/HGP.html
- Human Genome Project Information (Another valuable source of information on this research.)
  www.ornl.gov/TechResources/Human_Genome/home.html
- Human Population Genetics Laboratory (Luca Cavalli-Sforza's lab at Stanford University.)
  lotka.stanford.edu
- Phylogeny Programs (Online collection of over 120 computer programs for interpreting phylogenetic relationships.)
  evolution.genetics.washington.edu/phylip/software.html

- Race, Genes & Anthropology (Resource for the intepretation of "race.")
www-sul.stanford.edu/depts/ssrg/misc/race.html

Human Demography. The following are a few of the many sites that provide materials to support research on demography.

- Centers for Disease Control and Prevention (Online access to extensive information on current epidemics and disease studies.)
www.cdc.gov/cdc.htm
- U.S. Census Bureau (A remarkable quantity of census information is available online.)
www.census.gov
- World Health Organization (Information on disease and health from around the world.)
www.who.int

Cultural Anthropology

The study of human society and culture has been greatly facilitated by the ready access the Web provides to information about people around the world. There are a number of valuable applications of the medium of graphical browsers, not the least of which is the visual representation of people themselves. Other applications include tools for visual representation of kinship classification. The following is a sample of the kinds of sites that are available for learning about cultural anthropology.

- ANTHAP: The Applied Anthropology Computer Network
www.acs.oakland.edu/~dow/anthap.html
- The Anthropologist in the Field (Reference on ethnographic fieldwork by Laura Zimmer Tamakoshi using case study of Papua New Guinea.)
www.truman.edu/academics/ss/faculty/tamakoshil
- The Crees of Northern Quebec (Ethnographic project in visual anthropology. Photographic essay by Norman Chance and Paul Conklin.)
www.lib.uconn.edu/ArcticCircle/CulturalViability/Cree/creeexhibit.html
- Ethnic World Survey (Sponsored by the Centre Internacional Escarré per a les Minories Ètniques i Nacionals.)
www.partal.com/ciemen/ethnic.html
- Ethnomedicine Online Media Archive
www.med.uni-muenchen.de/medpsy/ethno/media-engl.html
- FIG: Folk Illness Glossary (Online guide to folk illnesses and related terminology. Includes links to other valuable resources for medical anthropology.)
ihs2.unn.ac.uk:8080/figit.htm

- History of Biomedicine (Extensive information on the history of medicine, including ancient Mesopotamian and Egyptian medicine, systems of Chinese, Indian, and Islamic traditional medicine as well as Western medicine. Includes many other valuable links from the Karolinska Institute.)
  www.mic.ki.se/History.html
- IQ and Race (Essay from *The Skeptic's Dictionary*.)
  wheel.ucdavis.edu/%7Ebtcarrol/skeptic/iq&race.html
- Kinship & Social Organization: Interactive Online Tutorial
  www.umanitoba.ca/faculties/arts/anthropology/kintitle.html
- Kinship Terminology (Hypertext guide to the systems used for classifying kinship and descent.)
  www.lib.uconn.edu/ArchNet/Topical/Educat/anth220/kinship.htm
- Links to Aboriginal Resources (Tremendous resource on indigenous peoples, created by Bill Henderson.)
  www.bloorstreet.com/300block/aborl.htm
- Race and Ethnicity (Valuable resource with lots of Web links.)
  www.Trinity.Edu/~mkearl/race.html
- Reflections on Fieldwork Among the Sinai Bedouin Women
  www.sherryart.com/women/bedouin.html
- What Is Culture?
  www.wsu.edu:8001/vcwsu/commons/topics/culture/culture-index.html
- WWW Virtual Library: Aboriginal Studies
  www.ciolek.com/WWWVL-Aboriginal.html
- WWW Virtual Library: Indigenous Studies
  www.halcyon.com/FWDP/wwwvl/indig-vl.html

Archaeology

There are several home pages that provide links to archaeological information. Each of these is just a starting point for exploration of the abundant materials about archaeological topics that are now available on the Web. One of the best starting points for an exploration of archaeology on the Web is ArchNet, an attractive site with effective navigation tools. You should also explore links provided by the several online archaeology courses, such as Introduction to Archaeology <www.ukans.edu/~hoopes/anth110.html>.

There is a great deal of information available online about specific archaeological sites, cultures, regions, and time periods. The best way to find this material is to make use of links from the sites listed below *and* to do searches on names of specific sites using online search engines. Simply type in the name of a site and see if you get any hits. Major sites that are open to the public, especially those with on-site museums, often have a presence on the Web. Sites that are maintained by the federal government (especially national monuments), by state governments, or by historical societies increasingly have dedicated Web sites. For example, the largest, near-urban, prehistoric site north of Mexico—Cahokia, in Illinois—has a terrific Web site <medicine.wustl.edu/~mckinney/cahokia/cahokia.html/> with maps, photographs, and a lot of narrative. Many of the well-known prehistoric Pueblo sites in the American Southwest are well represented on the Web; for examples, search on "Mesa Verde" or "Chaco Canyon." Other Web sites, such as the one for the Maya city of Caracol (Belize), have been developed by specific research projects.

- The Anasazi (Reference on the "ancient ones" of the Four Corners region of the southwestern United States.)
  www.afternet.com/~ray/c2/anasazi.html
- Ancient World Web (An enormous and excellent list of resources about ancient times, assembled by Julia Hayden.)
  www.julen.net/aw
- Archaeological Fieldwork Opportunities
  www.sscnet.ucla.edu/ioa/afs/testpit.html
- Archaeology (A list of links from the library at the University of Arizona.)
  dizzy.library.arizona.edu:80/users/jlcox/arch.html
- Archaeology on the Net (Index to many useful Web sites.)
  www.serve.com/archaeology
- Archaeology Resources for Education
  www.interlog.com/~jabram/elise/archres.htm
- ArchNet (Maintained by Thomas Plunkett and Jonathan Lizee, ArchNet features a wide variety of categories of site links. There is also a clickable map of world areas with links to hundreds of other Web sites.)
  spirit.lib.uconn.edu/ArchNet/ArchNet.html
- Comprehensive List of Archaeological Links (This is a long list, handily assembled by Lorelei Siegloff.)
  hal9000.net.au/~siegloff/arch/arch.html
- Ed Jolie's Home Page (Created by a high school student, this site offers a wide variety of links as well as a real-time chat forum for archaeology.)
  www.binary.net/edjolie
- Frequently Asked Questions About a Career in Archaeology in the U.S.
  www.museum.state.il.us/ismdepts/anthro/dlcfaq.html
- A Guide to Underwater Archaeology Resources on the Internet (Great information on sunken archaeological treasures.)
  www.pophaus.com/underwater
- Hal Rager's Archaeology Links
  www.nevada.edu/home/22/rager/pub/archae.html

- Links to the Past (A site developed by the U.S. National Park Service. It includes links to resources such as "Tools for Teaching" <www.cr.nps.gov/toolsfor.htm>, which provides basic information about archaeology for students and teachers.)
www.cr.nps.gov

- Mesoamerican Archaeology WWW Page (Valuable source of links for pre-Columbian studies across Latin America.)
copan.bioz.unibas.ch/meso.html

- Native American Archaeology & Anthropology Resources on the Internet (A huge list of links focusing on ancient peoples of the New World.)
hanksville.phast.umass.edu/misc/NAarch.html

- SARC–Stone Age Reference Collection (Source of information about early technology.)
www.hf.uio.no/iakn/roger/lithic/sarc.html

- The WWWorld of Archaeology
www.he.net/~archaeol/wwwarky/wwwarky.html

Online Course Materials. Archaeologists at a number of institutions have developed materials to support introductory and more specialized courses. Each of these provides a wealth of information and abundant links to information elsewhere on the Web, often arranged according to a course syllabus or schedule of lectures.

- Ancient American Civilizations: The Central Andes (Course materials developed by the author.)
www.ukans.edu/~hoopes/508

- Ancient American Civilizations: Mesoamerica (Course materials developed by the author.)
www.ukans.edu/~hoopes/506

- Anth 1602: Prehistoric Cultures (Award-winning Web site developed for a course by Tim Roufs at the University of Minnesota–Duluth. Includes a lot of worthwhile links.)
www.d.umn.edu/cla/faculty/troufs/anth1602

- Archaeology on Film (Electronic database of archaeology film reviews.)
www.sscf.ucsb.edu:80/anth/videos/video.html

- Archaeology: An Introduction (Supplement to Kevin Greene's 1995 textbook.)
www.ncl.ac.uk/~nktg/wintro

- Frequently Asked Questions About a Career in Archaeology in the U.S.
www.museum.state.il.us/ismdepts/anthro/dlcfaq.html

- Introduction to Archaeology (Developed by the author for a course at the University of Kansas, this award-winning site provides links, study guides, and sample tests organized as a semester-long undergraduate course.) www.ukans.edu/~hoopes/anth110.html
- Teaching Archaeometry (Course offered at the University of Illinois at Urbana-Champaign.) www.grad.uiuc.edu/departments/ATAM/teach-arch.html

Linguistics

The study of anthropological linguistics has substantial overlap with the study of linguistics as a discipline. The following URLs should be considered as starting points to an exploration of linguistics on the Web, with an emphasis on existing resources that deal specifically with language in social contexts.

- Language and Culture (Web site supporting Language-Culture, an online discussion for linguistic anthropology based at the University of Chicago.) <www.cs.uchicago.edu/l-c>
- Language and Linguistics Links (Large comprehensive index of information about linguistics on the Web. Maintained by Celso Alvarez Cáccamo—in Portuguese and English.) www.udc.es/dep/lx/linkseng.html
- Languages of the World (List of links to information about languages across the planet.) wwwcg.twi.tudelft.nl/~ari/lang.html
- Linganth Listserv Home Page (Web site supporting Linganth, a listserv for linguistic anthropology. Includes links to participants' Web sites.) www.beta-tech.com/linganth
- The LINGUIST List (Web site supporting LINGUIST, a major listserv for linguistics. An especially rich source of information, including an archive of past discussions.) www.emich.edu/~linguist
- The Mapuche Page (Information about the Mapuche, an indigenous people of southern Chile and Argentina. Maintained by Jennifer Arnold, a linguistic anthropologist at Stanford University.) www-linguistics.stanford.edu/~arnold/mapuche/mapuche-page.html
- Transcript of Mambila (Example of the potential of the Web for dissemination of research. Site provides a written transcript with audio recordings of Mambila speech by David Zeitlyn of the University of Kent.) rsl.ox.ac.uk/isca/mambila/mambila.html

- A Web of Online Dictionaries (Links to more than 330 dictionaries of over 100 different languages, including specialized technical and multilingual dictionaries. Includes search engine for English words in over 50 different dictionaries. Remarkable as a general reference source!) www.facstaff.bucknell.edu/rbeard/diction.html

- The World Wide Web Virtual Library: Linguistics (List of resources maintained by LINGUIST.) www.emich.edu/~linguist/www-vl.html

Creating Your Own Web Sites

The World Wide Web has made it possible for anyone to create useful resources that are accessible to a global audience. There are as many reasons for creating Web sites as there are individuals. You can create a personal home page to make it easier for people to find you, learn who you are, and communicate with you, or you can create a thematic page to provide access to information that you want to share. Keep in mind that Web resources are public and that anything you put on the Web is, in a sense, "published." The Web gives anyone the ability to run their own publishing house. It is a powerful medium, but it also comes with great responsibility. You will be held accountable for what you present online.

If you know how to use a word processor and a Web browser, you can learn how to create your own Web site. New software tools have made it possible to author and maintain professional-looking Web resources without any knowledge of HTML (hypertext markup language), the basic coding system for documents on the World Wide Web. In fact, the explosion of Web services has made it possible for anyone to develop a presence on the Web for free. You can now have an e-mail address and a Web site without even owning a computer!

A Web site is a collection of computer files that are stored in locations accessible via the World Wide Web. Because of the way the Web functions, the files do not even have to be on the same computer. A Web site with text, still images, animated images, audio, video, and even complex computer programs can be assembled from files spread all over the world. This collection of information is organized and presented via a series of HTML documents known as Web pages. The anchoring document is known as a home page, which provides an entrance (also conceived as a "gateway" or "portal") to hyperlinked resources. A Web site can consist of a single page or thousands of pages. It can be as simple as a few lines of text or as complex as a screenfull of frames, pull-down menus, pop-up dialog boxes, animated images, and automated links that lead to databases, movies, and computer programs written in languages like CGI (Common Gateway Interface), Java, and Active-X.

Writing Your Own HTML Code

To create a Web site, all you need is a text editor or word processor. To make it accessible to the world, you need a place where you can store this file on a computer (known as a server) that can be opened by browser software. A server can be a computer dedicated to providing Web access, or it can be just one of many programs running on a computer connected to the Internet.

The Web site itself begins with a plain text file (one without formatting by a word processor) that contains codes in HTML to instruct Web browsers how to display its contents. A simple version of a Web page might look like this:

```
<HTML>
<HEAD>
<META NAME="Author" CONTENT="My Name">
<META NAME = "Description" CONTENT = "What I know about
    anthropology.">
<META NAME = "Key words" CONTENT = "Anthropology">
</HEAD>
<BODY>
<CENTER><B><FONT SIZE=+2>My Anthropology Web
    Page</FONT></B></CENTER></HEAD>
<CENTER><A HREF="http://www.university.edu"><IMG
    SRC="image.jpg" HEIGHT=200 WIDTH=300></A></CENTER>
<CENTER>A simple line of text.</CENTER>
<CENTER>A simple <A HREF="http://www.university.edu">link</A>.
    </CENTER>
</BODY>
</HTML>
```

When displayed with browser software (such as Netscape Navigator or Microsoft Internet Explorer), this text file (named "sample.html") would display a title in boldface and larger than average size, an image linked to another Web page, a line of text, and a line of text with an embedded hypertext link. The text in capital letters enclosed by "< >" is an HTML tag. Note that these tags are in pairs, opening with a command in "< >" and closing with one in "</ >". To see how this works, replace the text between quotation marks and tags with your own information, save it to a file with the extension ".htm," and open it in a browser window.

Although writing your own HTML is the classic way to create a Web page, it can also be the most tedious. There are hundreds of HTML tags and variations, which can be learned only with a lot of study and experience, and the process has become more complicated as different software companies add their own variations. To get an idea of what complex HTML code looks like, use the "View > Page Source" option in your browser or save a Web page and open it in a text editor or word processor.

Most bookstores offer dozens of manuals on HTML. However, some of the best information on how to create a Web site is available on the Web itself. The following are a few of the good places to begin:

- Doc B's WebDesign Clinic (Step-by-step instruction on how to create an attractive Web site.)
  pages.prodigy.com/psych/wirdcli1.htm
- The HTML Guru (Resource with links to the latest information on HTML.)
  members.aol.com/htmlguru
- Wade's HTML Tutorial (Resource developed at MIT for teaching basic HTML commands.)
  web.mit.edu/afs/athena/user/w/s/wsmart/WEB/HTMLtutor.html
- WebMonkey Tutorial (Basic information on the use of HTML from the online magazine *HotWired!*)
  www.hotwired.com/webmonkey/teachingtool
- Yahoo! (Links to hundreds of sites with information on every aspect of Web page authoring.)
  www.yahoo.com/Computers_and_Internet/Internet/World_Wide_Web/Page_Creation

Authoring Tools

In the ancient days of computing, the first word processors required you to *manually* enter the codes for things like paragraph formatting, boldface, and italics within the text of a document. This is now done with hidden codes, automatically inserted by clicking, dragging, and so forth. Similarly, basic HTML coding has become automated in such a way that you can compose attractive pages without ever seeing (or writing) the HTML codes.

The latest versions of word processors such as Microsoft Word and Word-Perfect allow you to save a document in HTML format. This automatically inserts the basic tags necessary to display text and graphics and saves the file with the extension ".html" or ".htm" (allowing browsers to recognize it as an HTML file). Although the results are not always exactly what you might want, this is one of the fastest ways to create an attractive Web page. It also allows you to convert existing word processing documents to ones that can be incorporated into a Web site.

More sophisticated authoring tools can extend your ability to select colors and fancy backgrounds, insert graphics or audio files (such as background melody), wrap text around images, and even insert dialog boxes with pull-down menus. Tools for writing CGI scripts and Java programs can help you create fill-in-the-blank boxes for collecting information from visitors to your pages or providing access to behind-the-scenes databases and computer programs.

Among the most powerful and easy-to-use HTML authoring programs are Netscape Composer (part of the Netscape Communicator suite) and Microsoft Frontpage (part of the Microsoft Office suite). Versions of each of these are available free via downloading from the Web. In each, toolbars of icons and point-and-click or drag-and-drop commands make it easy to create Web pages with text, images, and links. Since versions of these programs are constantly being updated and improved, you should visit the manufacturer's Web sites to learn more about this software and how to use it.

- Netscape Composer (As a built-in component of the Netscape Communicator package, this is one of the most accessible Web page authoring tools around. It works seamlessly with Netscape Navigator to allow you to preview your pages as you work.)
www.netscape.com

- Microsoft Frontpage (Microsoft Frontpage Express is a free, smaller version of Microsoft Frontpage 98, one of the most powerful authoring tools available. The smaller version offers a number of useful features, including basic image editing capabilities. The full version is one of the best tools in existence for organizing and managing large Web sites.)
microsoft.com

A Picture Is Worth a Thousand Words

Hundreds of programs and devices are available for creating digitized drawings, photographs, backgrounds, pointers, and other types of visual displays. However, digitized image files must be in specific formats if they are to be included as parts of Web pages. These formats are known as GIFs (*.gif files) and JPEGs (*.jpg files). GIFs are most commonly used for backgrounds and small images, such as bullets, lines, and arrows. A special type of GIF can even display animation. JPEG files are compressed images that a browser can decompress and display, allowing for the display of large, high-resolution photographs with minimal downloading time. Most browser software can display either of these formats (to view an image file that's not in a Web page, simply "Open" it in your browser).

The easiest way to obtain GIF or JPEG files is to download them from the Web. There are hundreds of Web sites with free image files that you can use. To save a copy of an image in either Navigator or Internet Explorer, move the cursor over the image, click the right mouse button, and save the file to a directory. Remember that images are intellectual property, controlled by copyright laws. It is illegal to reproduce an image electronically without the permission of the copyright owner.

Another way to create images is with image processing software. One of the best examples is Adobe Photoshop <www.adobe.com>. However, if this is too expensive an option, free software is available for downloading off the Web. One site where it can be obtained is Shareware.com <shareware.com>. Search for an "Image Editor" and select a package that is designed for creating graphics for the Web.

Yet another way to obtain images is by using a peripheral device such as a camera, digital scanner, or video capture device. A scanner can be used to digitize photographs and illustrations. It can also make photographs of small three-dimensional objects (textiles, jewelry, seashells, etc.). Most scanners create TIFF files that must be converted to GIF or JPEG formats before they can be added to a Web page. Digital cameras create photographs that are already in digital formats that can be transferred to a computer for editing. If such a device is out of your price range, note that many photofinishing labs can give you copies of your own conventional photographs on floppy disks or even allow you to download them from a Web site.

Web Page Design Recommendations

There are about as many ways to design an Web site as there are individuals to create them. There are a few things to consider in making an attractive Web site:

Make it fast loading and easy to use. Long documents with big graphics files contribute to what many know as the "World Wide Wait." If your page takes a long time to scroll through, consider adding a menu of "targets" that point to specific locations within the page or breaking it up into a series of smaller, linked documents. Try to use small (< 100 KB) image files using compressed formats like JPEG.

Make it easy to get around. Include a lot of navigational buttons (graphic elements linked to targets or pages), especially ones that help a visitor get back to the beginning of the home page.

Make it nice to look at. One of the great advantages of the World Wide Web is that it is easy to format text information with fonts, colors, and images that hold a visitor's attention. Tables can be used in imaginative ways to organize both text and images. Many users find motion on a page to be distracting, so be conservative with flashing text or animated GIFs. Also, be sure that text can be read against any background graphics.

Warn about large downloads. If you are including a link to a big (> 100 KB) text, graphic, or audio file, it is courteous to let users know they might expect a wait. You should also advise them if they need any special plug-in software to view the file.

Avoid using too many frames. Many users prefer pages without frames, so consider offering a frameless version of your site.

Write labels for important graphics. Visitors who are using their browsers without images (for faster loading) will see only empty boxes unless you include verbal descriptions.

Test your site with different browsers. Some features do not appear the same way in Netscape, Microsoft, and other browsers. Try to avoid developing a site that works only with one browser.

Keep track of your visitors. Features like counters and guestbooks can help you to know whether your site is getting a lot of use and can be used to collect information about who is seeing your Web site.

Include an e-mail address so that users can contact you. This can be easily done using the "mailto:" prefix in front of your linked e-mail address. This is a valuable way to collect feedback and comments. You may even get tips about finding mistakes that you didn't catch yourself!

Web Site Hosting

Once you've created your HTML documents, you need a way to make them accessible to the world. The most common way to do this is to open an account on a server and create a "public_html" directory for a worldwide audience. (You should be able to find out how to do this from your university computer center.) Most university computer centers and commercial Internet service providers provide server space for Web site hosting. Policies, cost, and related services vary, so be sure to check with your provider to find out how to get a URL and how much server space you can access.

There are now at least 180 different sites on the World Wide Web that provide free server space for Web sites. Most also offer free e-mail as well as development tools—some of which can help you create an instant home page. A page listing several of these is offered by FreeWebspace.net <freewebspace.net>. Policies vary from one service to the next, but most prohibit the use of free server access for commercial purposes. Each of the services listed below provides sufficient storage space for a sophisticated Web site, with text, graphics, and room for other bells and whistles.

- Electric Minds (Founded by Web guru Howard Rheingold, this attractive site makes it easy to create and maintain a personal home page.) www.minds.com

- FreeYellow.com (Access to e-mail, 12 MB of storage space, and a host of useful development tools in return for the inclusion of advertising banners.) www.freeyellow.com

- Geocities (The most imaginative and successful of electronic communities, Geocities provides free e-mail addresses and server space for creating and

maintaining thematic Web sites. These are organized into virtual "neighborhoods" that also include real-time chat rooms.)
www.geocities.com

Development Resources

There are thousands of sites on the Web that can help you to develop and maintain an attractive and useful Web site. The following are a few examples:

- DesktopPublishing.com (An amazingly useful site with just about every tool one needs for electronic publishing. The "Web Designer's Paradise" page has hundreds of free graphics and tools for dressing up your site.)
desktoppublishing.com

- NetMechanic (This free and helpful service has tools to help you check for bad links and find bad HTML tags.)
www.netmechanic.com

- Web Pages That Suck (Learn how to design pages that work by looking at examples of ones that don't!)
www.webpagesthatsuck.com

- WS_FTP Limited Edition (An excellent tool for uploading and downloading files to and from an Internet server, available free to students, faculty, and noncommercial home users.)
www.ipswitch.com/downloads/ws_ftp_LE.html

- Yale Center for Advanced Instructional Media Web Style Guide (A sophisticated online manual with abundant information on how to create a first-class educational Web site.)
info.med.yale.edu/caim/manual

Promoting Your Web Site

There is little point to having a Web site that nobody ever sees. In order to get visitors to your site, there must be a way for people to find it. Once your site is on the Web, it will eventually be found by search engine "spiders" that prowl the Internet, indexing sites on the basis of content. One way to help these services know about the content of your site is to include key words after a META tag in the head of your HTML document. The more different terms you include, the more likely someone searching for a specific key word will find your page.

Contact Webmasters. A good way to promote your site's existence is to contact Webmasters (individuals who create and maintain other Web sites) and suggest that they include links from their pages to your own URL. For example, if you have created a Web site dedicated to information about racism, send e-mail to the Webmasters of other sites that address the same topic. One of the most common forms of cooperation on the Web is for Webmasters to reciprocate links with links from their own pages, which ultimately improves the interconnectedness of similar sites and pages. If you are at a college or university, request links to your site from a departmental Web site.

Contact newsgroups and listservs. An easy way to let a large number of people know about your Web site is to post a message about it to a Usenet newsgroup or a topical listserv. One thing you should not do, however, is generate "spam"—multiple copies of unsolicited e-mail messages.

Get listed on search engines. You can submit URLs directly to most search engines. Once your page is online, go to the home pages for Yahoo!, AltaVista, Excite, Lycos, and other services and follow the links on how to submit URLs.

Join Web rings. Another fun way to generate visits to your site is to join a "ring" of serially linked Web sites. Two excellent examples follow:

- The Paleo Ring (Currently links over 170 Web sites on topics pertaining to archaeology and paleontology.)
  www.pitt.edu/~mattf/PaleoRing.html

- Anthropology Web Ring (Dedicated to topical sites in anthropology.)
  www.serve.com/archaeology/anthring

Future Directions

The Internet is a dynamic and constantly changing environment. There is no doubt that new developments in software, hardware, and the social contexts in which these are used will result in constant and radical changes in the way this medium is used. At present, most of the resources are based on static text and image files. We can expect, however, a rapid increase in the use of animated images and both audio and video recordings. There will also be a rapid increase in the number and variety of interactive resources, from chat rooms, to 3D "virtual worlds," to full-duplex video conferences.

Along with new forms of multimedia communication, we can anticipate a significant increase in both the quantity and quality of information that is accessible online. The ability to utilize this information will ultimately depend on better search engines and indexes.

Cool Sites

The following are just a few examples of projects representative of the new media and new directions of interest to anthropologists that are offered by the Internet. Perhaps these, as well as the resources listed previously, will inspire you to create your own presence on the Web!

Ethnic Music Sources
Digital audio sources have made it easier than ever to enjoy and learn about the music of other cultures. Many Web sites now offer either downloadable audio files or streaming audio broadcasts. There are hundreds of resources for ethnic

music from around the world. The following is just a sampler. (Note: You will need to have a sound card, headphones or speakers, and the appropriate audio plug-in software for your browser to be able to enjoy music off the Web.)

- African Music (List of links from the University of Illinois.)
  www.soc.uiuc.edu/soc122/music.htm
- African Music Archive (From the Institute of Ethnology and African Studies, Johannes Gutenberg University, Mainz, Germany.)
  www.uni-mainz.de/~bender
- The Arabic Music Page
  leb.net/rma
- Ceolas (Resource for Celtic music.)
  www.ceolas.org/ceolas.html
- The Chinese Music Page
  vizlab.rutgers.edu/~jaray/sounds/chinese_music/chinese_music.html
- The Jewish Music Network
  www.jewish-music.com
- Marco Polo Chinese Jukebox
  www.hnh.com/rahome/rampc.htm
- La Musica.com! (Definitive source of information on music from Latin America.)
  www.lamusica.com
- Native American Music Resources on the Internet
  hanksville.phast.umass.edu/misc/NAmusic.html
- Peruvian Music
  ekeko.rcp.net.pe/snd/snd_ingles.html
- Seven Colors of the Baltics (Traditional music of the Balkans.)
  www.geocities.com/Vienna/3651
- Yahoo! (Listing of "world music" Web sites by countries, cultures, and ethnic groups.)
  www.yahoo.com/Entertainment/Music/Countries_Cultures_and_Groups/

Virtual Reality

Two of the techniques that have been developed to provide three-dimensional imagery on the Web are Apple's Quicktime VR and VRML (a virtual reality coding language). With the right software, images on the screen can be turned and manipulated in three dimensions, allowing for the exploration of simulated spaces. Each of the following sites is an excellent example of the application of these techniques to anthropological data. One can only imagine what the next generation of 3D technology will be able to do. . . .

- Cerén (Spectacular 3D reconstructions of an ancient Maya village in El Salvador.)
  wallstreet.colorado.edu/projects/projects.html
- Chetro Ketl Great Kiva (One of the first Quicktime VR projects in archaeology on the Web. Impressive 3D reconstruction of a sacred kiva of the Anasazi people from the southwestern United States. Includes audio files and 3D images of ancient pottery.)
  sipapu.ucsb.edu/html/kiva.html
- Virtual Stonehenge (VRML model of Stonehenge, a Neolithic site in England that has been associated with astronomical observations.)
  www.tms.nl/vrtscedu.htm
- Yaxuna Archaeology (Presentation of research at the site of Yaxuna, a Maya town in the northern Yucatán peninsula. Has lots of Quicktime VR images from the project that allow you to feel as if you were visiting the site and having a look around.)
  tesla.csuhayward.edu/sacredplaces/yaxuna.html

Tele-Embodiment
Tours of virtual reality are complemented by virtual tours of reality. The following are a few of the projects that seek to turn Web browsers into movable windows on events happening in the real world—and give users an opportunity to change them!

- The Mercury Project (The first installation to combine robotics and Web access to simulate an archaeological investigation.)
  www.usc.edu/dept/raiders
- Personal Roving Presence (PRoP) (Prototypes of floating robotic devices, programmable via the Web. Someday, these devices will permit individuals to boldly go where no one has gone before. . . .)
  www.prop.org

Just a small amount of Internet surfing should make it apparent that this global network is filled with a rapidly expanding universe of valuable information about all areas of anthropology. This body of information will only increase as more anthropologists and their students learn how to create resources themselves and make them available to a growing worldwide audience. How these materials are used will be a measure of the creativity and resourcefulness of individual instructors and their students. However, there are also some cautions to keep in mind. For one, the Internet will always supplement, and never replace, traditional library resources for anthropology. It is impossible to do thorough research using only what is available on the Web. It is also likely to be several years before Internet access is as durable, portable, and useful as a good textbook. Another issue has to do with the ease with which Internet resources are created. It is just as easy to put faulty, misleading, and harmful information on the Web as it is to put good scholarship there. Critical thinking skills and the ability to evaluate qualities such as bias, point of view, and authority are essential for intelligent learning in any context. Just because something *looks* professional and authoritative does not mean it is. There is a lot of information on the Internet that is far worse than worthless—information that promotes ignorance, misunderstanding, hate, and even violence. With the exception of Usenet newsgroups (which remain fraught with problems), an attempt has been made to include here only those resources that are considered reliable from an academically informed perspective. However, there are many paths that may lead to hazardous ends. *Caveat internauta!* (Surfer beware!)

INTERNET GLOSSARY

Archie   A search engine for anonymous FTP archives.

ArchiePlex   Web-based interface for using Archie.

bandwidth   The amount of information that can be transferred across a network at one time.

bit   The smallest unit of information in a computer; represented by 0 or 1.

bookmark   A tool provided by most Web browsers that enables you to save Web-page URLs so that you can return to them at any time.

Boolean logic   A system for searching a database that uses the operators AND, OR, and NOT to look for two variables.

bps   A measure of data transmission capacity, used to describe a modem's speed, such as 28.8K bps (or 28,800 bits per second).

browser   An interface for reading information on the World Wide Web, either graphical (such as Netscape or Explorer) or textual (such as Lynx).

bulletin board (BBS)   Area where users can read and post messages, as well as download files.

byte   A unit of information in a computer, equal to 8 bits.

CD-ROM   (compact disk, read-only memory) A compact disk used to store and retrieve computer data.

chat   Electronic conversations among Internet users taking place in real time in chat areas (or chat channels, groups, rooms, or sites).

client   The computer and software you use to access Internet servers.

DNS (domain name system)   The convention for translating the names of hosts into Internet addresses; see also **URL**.

domain name   The part of the Internet address (URL) that specifies the area on a computer reserved for a particular organization, such as mayfieldpub. com. In this example, .com stands for "commercial"; other types of organization designations include .edu for "educational" and .gov for "governmental."

download   To transfer information from one computer to another, or to transfer information from a network to your computer.

e-mail   Electronic mail; one of the most popular uses of the Internet; it can be sent to an individual or a list.

FAQs (frequently asked questions)   Lists of common questions about a particular product, service, or topic.

file path   Subdirectory in a URL, leading to the specific file you want.

flaming   Sending angry messages, usually to someone who has broken the rules of netiquette.

freeware   Copyrighted software that is distributed for free and may not be resold.

FTP (file transfer protocol)   The standard protocol for transferring files across the Internet.   Most browsers have one-way FTP; for two-way (the ability to send as well as receive), you can acquire FTP software for both Macintoshes (Fetch) and PCs (WS_FTP).

GIF (graphics interchange format)   File format for compressed images that are viewable on the Web that is designed to minimize data loss. GIFs are best used for flat color images; see also **JPEG**.

Gopher   A menu-driven information system created at the University of Minnesota.

hits   The number of times a particular page is accessed, or the number of successful matches you receive during a key word search.

home page   The main, or starting, page for a series of Web pages.

HTML (hypertext markup language)   The formatting language of the World Wide Web.

HTTP (hypertext transfer protocol)   The protocol for reading HTML programs from the Web.

hyperlink   See **link**.

hypermedia   Links among various kinds of multimedia objects, such as video, audio, and virtual reality, in addition to text and graphics.

hypertext   A text link that takes you to another file on the Internet. A hypertext document contains hypertext or hyperlinks or both.

Internet   A global network of linked computers; home to the World Wide Web, newsgroups, bulletin boards, Gopher, and online forums.

IRC (Internet relay chat)   See **chat**.

ISP (Internet service provider)   A company that provides subscribers access to the Internet.

JPEG or **JPG** (joint photographic expert group)   File format for compressed images that are viewable on the Web that is designed to lose original data in order to make a small file. JPEGs work best on large complex images; see also **GIF**.

Jughead   A search engine for Gopher document titles.

link   Short for *hyperlink*. A link, textual or graphic, that takes you to another file on the Internet or another location in a document.

listserv   A program that distributes e-mail to a mailing list.

lurk   To browse and read messages, but not actively participate in a discussion group. It's a good idea to lurk before joining discussion groups.

mailing list   A discussion group that shares an interest in a particular topic; messages sent by members of the group are e-mailed to all its members.

modem   A device that allows a remote computer to communicate via phone lines to networks and other computers.

MOO (MUD object-oriented environment)   Multi-user environment based on object-oriented programming technology. See **MUD**.

MUD (multi-user domain [dungeon or dimension]) Virtual environment on the Internet primarily used for role-playing games such as Dungeons and Dragons.

MUSH (multi-user shared hallucination) A MUD variation.

netiquette Etiquette on the Internet. The guidelines for preferred behavior when communicating with others on the Internet.

network A system of computers that can transmit information from one to another.

newsgroup A discussion group, or informal bulletin board, that shares an interest in a particular topic; newsgroups are located on Usenet, where articles are read and posted.

packet When information is transferred from the Internet to your computer, it is broken into pieces, or packets, which are transmitted to your computer and reassembled by TCP software.

POP (post office protocol) The standard protocol for reading Internet mail sent using SMTP.

protocol Information format. The protocol lets two computers know what type of information is being transferred. The protocol for transferring information across the Internet is given in the first part of the URL (e.g., http, ftp, gopher, telnet).

proxy server A server that sits between a real server and a browser (or other client application) and functions as the real server.

RAM (random access memory) The amount of available short-term memory in a computer directly correlates to the speed of your processor—the more RAM you have, the faster your computer is.

ROM (read-only memory) The unchangeable portion of the computer's memory containing the start-up instructions for your system.

search engine A program that allows you to perform key word searches to locate documents.

server A computer accessible to other networked computers.

shareware Copyrighted software that is distributed on a trial basis; you eventually have to pay for it if you want to continue to use it beyond the trial period. The cost is generally minimal.

SMTP (simple mail transfer protocol) The standard protocol for transferring e-mail from one computer to another across the Internet.

spam Unsolicited e-mail usually sent to a large number of users, such as to a Usenet group or a listserv mailing list.

subject tree A hierarchical directory of information.

surfing Aimlessly exploring the Internet by clicking links from one page to another.

tags Codes used in hypertext markup language (HTML).

TCP/IP (transmission control protocol/Internet protocol) TCP is the software your computer uses to create an interface with the Internet. TCP software receives the packets of data transmitted across the Internet and reassembles the corresponding file so that you can view the resulting Web page. IP is the protocol that computers use to talk to each other on the Internet, and it helps to define the route packets take.

Telnet   A standard protocol for logging on to another computer remotely. For example, if you want to log on from home to your UNIX account at school, you can use Telnet.

thread   The original newsgroup message (article) and all of its associated replies.

TIFF (tagged information file format)   File format for storing greyscale or color images on PC and Macintosh computers. Not viewable on the Web.

UNIX   A freeware computer operating system used by many colleges and universities.

URL (uniform resource locator)   An address for an Internet location.

Usenet   A UNIX-based computing system used mainly for discussion and newsgroups.

Veronica   A program that searches the full text of Gopher documents.

videoconference   Two or more people interacting through real-time video and audio feeds.

virus   A self-replicating destructive program that can be downloaded from the Internet or obtained via an infected file on a diskette. A few viruses are harmless and even amusing, but most can destroy the data on your hard disk.

Web page   Any Web document viewable with a browser.

World Wide Web   The segment of the Internet that uses primarily HTTP.

WOO (Web object-oriented environment)   A virtual space primarily used for role-playing similar to a MUD, but located on the World Wide Web.

INDEX

Active-X, 66
AltaVista, 7, 8, 9, 26, 37, 39, 45
American Psychological Association
  (APA), 15, 18, 19, 39
angle brackets, 2, 3, 17, 36, 67
anthropology Internet resources
  archaeology, 62–64
  cultural, 61–62
  ethnic music sources, 73–74
  human demography, 61
  human evolution, 58–59
  human genetics and
    biological diversity, 60–61
  journals and online
    publications, 56–58
  library research, 53–54
  linguistics, 65–66
  links, 51–53
  listservs, 48–50
  museums, 54–55
  newsgroups, 47–50
  online course material, 53–54, 58,
    64–65
  physical/biological, 58–59
  primate studies, 59–60
  professional societies, 55–56
  virtual reality, 74–75
  Usenet sites, 47–48
Archie, 7, 30, 77
ArchiePlex, 7, 30, 77
Auto Load Images, 37

bandwidth, 7, 77
bit, 4, 77
bookmark, 2, 51, 77
Boolean logic, 7, 46, 77
bps, 4, 77
browser, 2, 3, 4, 5, 6, 7, 10, 11, 24, 27,
  30, 37, 38, 51, 77

bulletin board, 11, 51, 77
byte, 4, 77

CD-ROM, 14, 17, 19, 21, 23, 77
CGI, 66
changeable sources, 14, 17, 19, 21, 23
chat, 28, 30, 48, 77
chat room, 28, 72, 73
Chicago Manual of Style (CMS), 15, 22, 23
client, 5, 28, 29, 77
copyright, 13, 24, 31, 39–40
Council of Biological Editors (CBE), 15,
  20, 21
credibility, 8, 13
CU-SeeMe, 29

direct quotations, 15
discussion groups, 24, 26, 47–48
DNS (domain name system), 10, 77
documenting sources, 14, 15–23
domain name, 5, 25, 29, 31, 45, 77
download, 1, 4, 6, 11, 24, 28, 29, 30, 31,
  32, 37, 42, 77

electronic-source citations, 14, 15, 16, 17,
  18, 19, 20, 21, 22, 23
e-mail, 1, 6, 7, 13, 24, 25, 26, 27, 28, 29,
  30, 31, 34, 37, 46, 48, 49, 51, 66, 71,
  72, 73, 77
error messages, 10, 51
Explorer, 2, 4, 7, 24, 27, 30, 67, 69
Excite, 45

fair use, 28
FAQ (Frequently Asked Questions), 11,
  26, 28, 29, 77
file path, 5–6, 77
file transfer, 1, 6. *See also* FTP
flaming, 26, 47, 48, 77

FAVORITE WEB SITES

Name of Site: _____

URL: _____

Name of Site: _____

URL: _____

Name of Site: _____

URL: _____

Name of Site: _____

URL: _____

Name of Site: _____

URL: _____

Name of Site: _____

URL: _____

Name of Site: _____

URL: _____

Name of Site: _____

URL: _____

Name of Site: _____

URL: _____

Name of Site: _____

URL: _____

Name of Site: _____

URL: _____

Name of Site: _____

URL: _____

Name of Site: _____

URL: _____

Name of Site: _____

URL: _____

Name of Site: _____

URL: _____

Name of Site: _____

URL: _____

Name of Site: _____

URL: _____

Name of Site: _____

URL: _____

Name of Site: _____

URL: _____

Name of Site: _____

URL: _____

Name of Site: _____

URL: _____

Name of Site: _____

URL: _____

Name of Site: _____

URL: _____

Name of Site: _____

URL: _____

Name of Site: _____

URL: _____

Name of Site: _____

URL: _____

Name of Site: _____

URL: _____

Name of Site: _____

URL: _____

Name of Site: _____

URL: _____

Name of Site: _____

URL: _____

Name of Site: _____

URL: _____

Name of Site: _____

URL: _____

Name of Site: _____

URL: _____

Name of Site: _____

URL: _____

Name of Site: _____

URL: _____

Name of Site: _____

URL: _____

Name of Site: _____

URL: _____

Name of Site: _____

URL: _____

Name of Site: _____

URL: _____

Name of Site: _____

URL: _____

Name of Site: _____

URL: _____

Name of Site: _____

URL: _____

Name of Site: _____

URL: _____

Name of Site: _____

URL: _____

Name of Site: _____

URL: _____

Name of Site: _____

URL: _____

Name of Site: _____

URL: _____

Name of Site: _____

URL: _____

Name of Site: _____

URL: _____

Name of Site: _____

URL: _____

Name of Site: _____

URL: _____

Name of Site: _____

URL: _____

Name of Site: _____

URL: _____

Name of Site: _____

URL: _____

Name of Site: _____

URL: _____

Name of Site: _____

URL: _____

Name of Site: _____

URL: _____

Name of Site: _____

URL: _____

Name of Site: _____

URL: _____

Name of Site: _____

URL: _____

Name of Site: _____

URL: _____

Name of Site: _____

URL: _____

Name of Site: _____

URL: _____

Name of Site: _____

URL: _____

Name of Site: _____

URL: _____

Name of Site: _____

URL: _____

Name of Site: _____

URL: _____

Name of Site: _____

URL: _____

Name of Site: _____

URL: _____

Name of Site: _____

URL: _____

Name of Site: _____

URL: _____

Name of Site: _____

URL: _____

Name of Site: _____

URL: _____

Name of Site: _____

URL: _____

Name of Site: _____

URL: _____

Name of Site: _____

URL: _____